SUZUKI
380-750cc TRIPLES • 1972-1977
SERVICE • REPAIR • PERFORMANCE

ERIC JORGENSEN
Editor

JEFF ROBINSON
Publisher

CLYMER PUBLICATIONS

World's largest publisher of books devoted exclusively to
automobiles and motorcycles.

12860 MUSCATINE STREET • P.O. BOX 20 • ARLETA, CALIFORNIA 91331

MOTORCYCLE INDUSTRY COUNCIL

CONTENTS

QUICK REFERENCE DATA

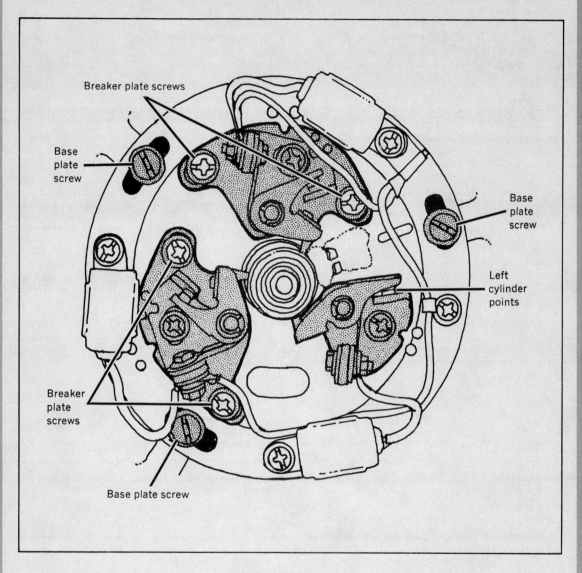

Breaker plate screws

Base plate screw

Base plate screw

Left cylinder points

Breaker plate screws

Base plate screw

IGNITION SPECIFICATIONS

	in.	(mm)		in.	(mm)
Breaker point gap	0.014	(0.35)	GT380 L	0.094	(2.40)
Spark plug gap	0.028	(0.7)	GT380 M	0.090 0.088	(2.30)* (2.25)**
Ignition timing (distance BTDC)			GT550	0.132	(3.37)
GT380 A, B	0.082 0.080	(2.09)* (2.05)**	GT750 J, K, L, M	0.143 0.134	(3.64)* (3.42)**
GT380 J, K	0.117 0.115	(2.99)* (2.93)**	GT750 A, B	0.142 0.134	(3.63)* (3.42)**

* Right and left cylinders ** Center cylinder

IDLE MIXTURE ADJUSTMENT

Model	Turns
GT380	1¼
GT550 J, K	1¼
GT550 (all others)	1½
GT750 J, K	1½
GT750 L	¼
GT750 M, A, B	¾

NOTE: Tolerance for adjustments is ± ¼ turn.
Adjust for smoothest idle.

BATTERY APPLICATION

GT380 B; GT550 K, L, M, A, B	12N11-3A-1
GT550 J	12N11-3B
GT380 J, K, L, M, A	12N7-4A
GGT750	12N14-3A

SPARK PLUG APPLICATION

Model	NGK	ND	Champion
GT380 J, K	B-7ES	W22ES	N3-MC
GT550 J, K, L	B-7ES	W22ES	N3-MC
GT750 J, K	B-7ES	W22ES	N3-MC
GT380 L, M, A, B	B-8ES	W24ES	N2-MC
GT550 M, A, B	B-8ES	W24ES	N2-MC
GT750 M, A, B	B-8ES	W24ES	N2-MC
GT750 L	B-6ES	W20ES	N4-MC

ADJUSTMENTS

Throttle cable free play	VM carburetors — 0.04 in. (1mm); BS carburetors — 0.1-0.2 in. (2-3mm) cable slack between adjuster and pulley on carburetor
Clutch lever free play	0.12 in. (3mm) free play at at handlebar lever
Drive chain free play	0.6-0.8 in. (15-20mm)
Front drum brake lever-to-grip	0.8-1.2 in. (20-30mm)
Rear brake pedal free play	0.8-1.2 in. (20-30mm)

RECOMMENDED FUEL AND LUBRICANTS

Engine oil	Suzuki CCI oil or good quality 2-cycle SAE 90 motorcycle oil
Transmission oil	Suzuki transmission oil or SAE 20/40 oil
Front forks	SAE 10 W/30 oil, ATF (automatic transmission fluid), or special front fork oil
Drive chain	SAE 30 oil or special chain lubricant
Fuel	Low-lead or non-lead gasoline 85-95 (research) octane

CAPACITIES

Model		Transmission			Front Fork (each leg)		
	cc	U.S. pt.	Imp. pt.		cc	U.S. oz.	Imp. oz.
GT380 J, K	1400	2.9	2.5		210	7.1	5.9
GT380 (all others)	1500	3.2	2.6		145	4.9	4.1
GT550 J, K, L	1500	3.2	2.6		235	7.9	6.6
GT550 (all others)	1500	3.2	2.6		160	5.4	4.5
GT750 J, K	2200	4.6	3.9		235	7.9	6.6
GT750 (all others)	2200	4.6	3.9		160	5.4	4.5

CHAPTER ONE

GENERAL INFORMATION

This book provides complete service and repair information for owners of Suzuki triple cylinder motorcycles. The contents apply to the GT380, GT550, and GT750.

SERVICE HINTS

Most of the service procedures described in this book are straightforward, and can be performed by anyone who is reasonably handy with tools. It is suggested however, that you consider your own capabilities carefully before you attempt any operation which involves major disassembly of the engine. Some operations, for example, require the use of a press. It would be wiser to have those operations performed by a shop equipped for such work, rather than to try to do the job yourself with makeshift equipment. Some procedures require precision measurements. Unless you have the skills and equipment to make these measurements, it would be better to have a motorcycle shop make them for you.

You will find that repairs will go much faster and easier if your machine is clean before you begin work. There are special cleaners for washing the engine and related parts. Just brush or spray on the cleaning solution, let it stand, then rinse it away with a garden hose. Clean all oily or greasy parts with cleaning solvent as you remove them. *Never use gasoline as a cleaning agent.* Gasoline presents an extreme fire hazard. Be sure to work in a well ventilated area when you use cleaning solvent. Keep a fire extinguisher, rated for gasoline fires, handy just in case.

Special tools are required for some service procedures. These tools may be purchased at Suzuki dealers. If you are on good terms with the dealer's service department, you may be able to use his.

Much of the labor charge for repairs made by dealers is for removal and disassembly of other parts to reach the defective one. It is frequently possible for you to do all of this yourself, then take the affected subassembly into the dealer for repair.

Once you decide to tackle the job yourself, read the entire section in this manual which pertains to the job. Study the illustrations and the text until you have a good idea of what is involved. If special tools are required, make arrangements to get them before you start the job. It is frustrating to get partly into a job and then find that you are unable to complete it.

TOOLS

Every motorcyclist should carry a small tool kit with him, to help make minor roadside adjustments or repairs. A suggested kit, available at most dealers, is shown in **Figure 1**.

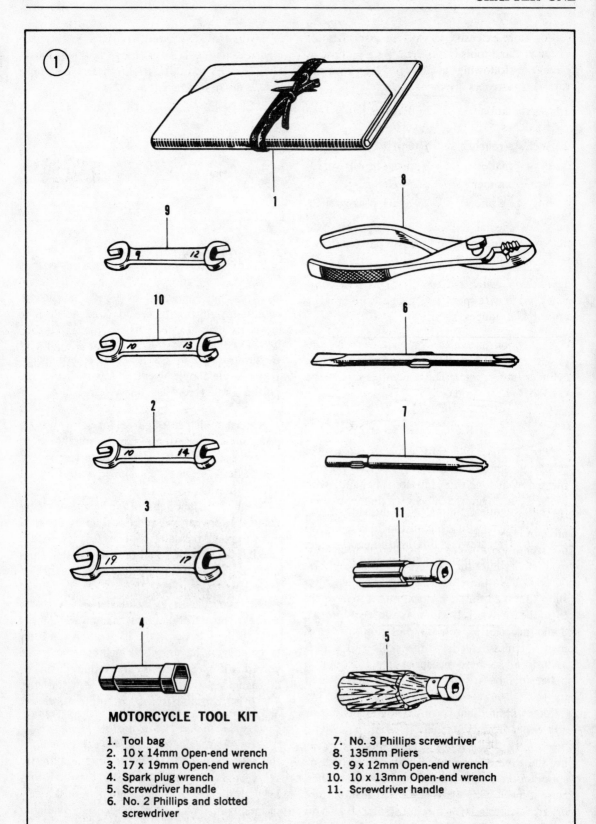

MOTORCYCLE TOOL KIT

1. Tool bag
2. 10 x 14mm Open-end wrench
3. 17 x 19mm Open-end wrench
4. Spark plug wrench
5. Screwdriver handle
6. No. 2 Phillips and slotted screwdriver
7. No. 3 Phillips screwdriver
8. 135mm Pliers
9. 9 x 12mm Open-end wrench
10. 10 x 13mm Open-end wrench
11. Screwdriver handle

For more extensive service, an assortment of ordinary hand tools is required. As a minimum, have the following available. Note that all threaded fasteners are metric sizes.

1. Combination wrenches
2. Socket wrenches
3. Plastic mallet
4. Small hammer
5. Snap ring pliers
6. Phillips screw-drivers
7. Pliers
8. Slot screwdrivers
9. Feeler gauges
10. Spark plug wrench

A few special tools are also required. The first few are inexpensive, and will pay for themselves very quickly.

1. *Ignition gauge* (**Figure 2**). This tool combines round wire spark plug gauges with breaker point feeler gauges.

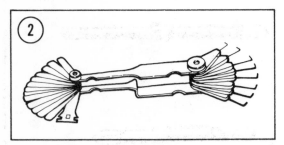

2. *Timing gauge* (**Figure 3**). Suzuki bikes require that ignition timing be set individually for each cylinder, with each piston in a specified position. By screwing this instrument in each spark plug hole, piston position may be determined easily.

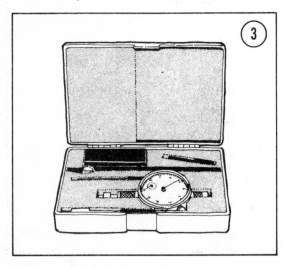

3. *Hydrometer* (**Figure 4**). This instrument measures battery state of charge, and tells much about battery condition. Hydrometers are available at all auto parts stores.

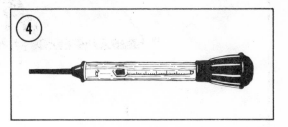

4. *Multimeter, or VOM* (**Figure 5**). This instrument is invaluable for electrical system troubleshooting and service. A few of its functions may be duplicated by locally fabricated substitutes, but for the serious hobbyist, it is a must. Its uses are described in the applicable sections of this book. Prices start at around $10 at electronics hobbyist stores and mail order outlets.

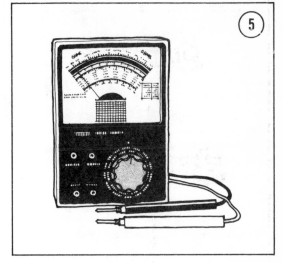

5. *Compression gauge* (**Figure 6**). An engine with low compression cannot be properly tuned and will not develop full power. The compression gauge shown has a flexible stem, which enables it to reach cylinders where there is little clearance between the cylinder head and frame.

6. *Impact driver* (**Figure 7**). This tool might have been designed with the motorcyclist in mind. It makes removal of engine cover screws easy, and eliminates damaged screw slots.

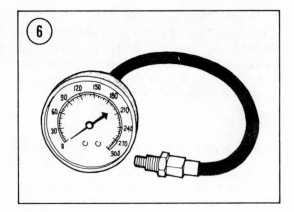

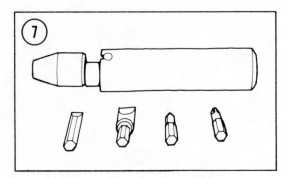

EXPENDABLE SUPPLIES

Certain expendable supplies are also required. These include grease, oil, gasket cement, wiping rags, cleaning solvent, and distilled water. Cleaning solvent is available at many service stations. Distilled water, required for battery service, is available at every supermarket. It is sold for use in steam irons, and is quite inexpensive.

MECHANIC'S TIPS

Removing Frozen Nuts and Screws

When a fastener rusts and cannot be removed, several methods may be used to loosen it. First apply penetrating oil liberally. Rap the fastener several times with a small hammer; do not hit it hard enough to cause damage.

For frozen screws, apply oil as described, then insert a screwdriver in the slot and rap the top of the screwdriver with a hammer. This loosens the rust so the screw can be removed in the normal way. If the screw head is too chewed up to use a screwdriver, grip the head with vise-type pliers and turn the screw out.

For a frozen bolt or nut, apply penetrating oil, then rap it with a hammer. Turn it off with the proper size wrench. If the points are rounded off, grip with vise-type pliers as described for screws.

Stripped Threads

Occasionally, threads are stripped through carelessness or impact damage. Often the threads can be cleaned up by running a tap (for internal threads) or die (for external threads) through the threads. See **Figure 8**.

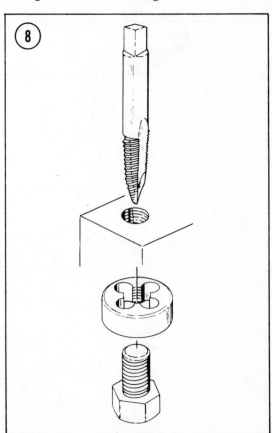

Broken Screw or Bolt

When the head breaks off a screw or bolt, several methods are available for removing the remaining portion.

If a large portion of the remainder projects out, try gripping it with vise-type pliers. If the projecting portion is too small, try filing it to fit a wrench or cut a slot in it to fit a screwdriver. See **Figure 9**.

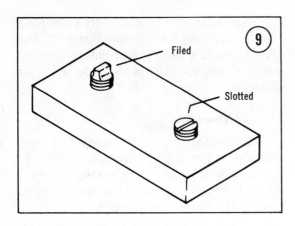

If the head breaks off flush, as it usually does, remove it with a screw extractor. Refer to **Figure 10**. Center-punch the broken part, then drill a hole into it. Drill sizes are marked on the tool. Tap the extractor into the broken part, then back it out with a wrench.

Removing Damaged Screws

> **WARNING**
> *When removing screws by this method, always wear suitable eye protection.*

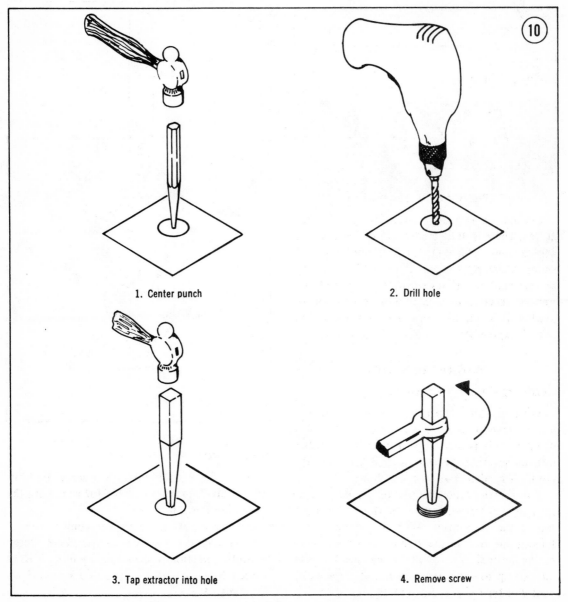

1. Center punch

2. Drill hole

3. Tap extractor into hole

4. Remove screw

CAUTION
Use clean rags to cover bearings or
any other parts which might be harmed
by metal chips produced during this
procedure.

Figure 11 illustrates damaged screws typical
of those on many bikes. Such screws may usually be removed easily by drilling. Select a bit
with a diameter larger than that of the damaged
screw, but smaller than its head, then drill into
the screw head (**Figure 12**) until the head sepa-
rates from the screw. The remainder of the
screw may then be turned out easily. **Figure 13**
illustrates one screw head removed in this manner. The other has been drilled to just the point
where the head is separating from the screw
body. Note that there is no damage to the plate
which these screws retain.

SAFETY FIRST

Professional mechanics can work for years
without sustaining serious injury. If you observe
a few rules of common sense and safety, you can
also enjoy many safe hours servicing your own
machine. You can also hurt yourself or damage
the bike if you ignore these rules.

1. Never use gasoline as a cleaning solvent.

2. Never smoke or use a torch near flammable
liquids, such as cleaning solvent in open
containers.

3. Never smoke or use a torch in an area where
batteries are charging. Highly explosive hydrogen gas is formed during the charging process.

4. If welding or brazing is required on the
machine, remove the fuel tank to a safe distance, at least 50 feet away.

5. Be sure to use proper size wrenches for
nut turning.

6. If a nut is tight, think for a moment what
would happen to your hand should the wrench
slip. Be guided accordingly.

7. Keep your work area clean and uncluttered.

8. Wear safety goggles in all operations involv-
ing drilling, grinding, or use of a chisel.

9. Never use worn tools.

10. Keep a fire extenguisher handy. Be sure that
it is rated for gasoline and electrical fires.

CHAPTER TWO

2

PERIODIC MAINTENANCE

To obtain the utmost in safety, reliability, and performance from your motorcycle, it is necessary to perform periodic inspections, adjustments, and maintenance procedures. Frequently, minor problems found during such inspections are simple and inexpensive to correct at the time, but could lead to major failures later. This chapter describes such services.

Table 1 is a suggested maintenance schedule. Note that under more severe riding conditions some maintenance items may require attention more frequently.

ENGINE TUNE-UP

The number of definitions of the term "tune-up" is probably equal to the number of people defining it. For purposes of this book, we will define a tune-up as a general adjustment and/or service of all scheduled maintenance items to ensure continued peak operating efficiency of a motorcycle engine. As part of a proper tune-up, some service procedures are essential. The following paragraphs discuss details of these procedures.

Compression Test

An engine needs 3 basics to develop full power—proper fuel mixture, properly timed

Table 1   MAINTENANCE SCHEDULE

Service Item	Initial 500	Miles Thereafter 1,000	Miles Thereafter 2,000
Change oil	X		X
Check electrical equipment	X	X	
Service breaker points	X		X
Spark plugs	X	X	
Adjust ignition timing	X		X
Service air cleaner			X
Adjust oil pump	X		X
Adjust clutch	X		X
Remove carbon			X
Clean exhaust system			X
Clean fuel strainer			X
Check brakes	X	X	
Check chain	X	X	
Check spokes	X	X	
Tighten all fasteners	X		X
Grease chassis		X	

spark, and adequate compression. If for any reason compression is low, the engine will not develop full power. A compression test, or even better, a series of them over the life of the bike, will tell much about engine condition.

To make a compression test, proceed as follows.

1. Start the engine, then ride the bike long enough to warm it thoroughly.

2. Remove all spark plugs.

3. Screw the compression gauge into one spark plug hole, or if a press-in type gauge is used, hold it firmly in position.

4. With the throttle fully open, operate the kickstarter briskly several times; the compression gauge indication will increase with each kick. Continue to crank the engine until the gauge indicates no more increase, then record the compression gauge indication.

Example:

1st kick	50 psi
2nd kick	80 psi
3rd kick	90 psi
4th kick	100 psi
5th kick	100 psi

5. Repeat this procedure for each remaining cylinder.

Because of differences in individual engines, compression gauges, and various other factors, no definite compression pressures can be specified for any one engine. However, a series of measurements made over a period of time may reveal trouble ahead, long before the engine exhibits serious symptoms. Consider this example (**Table 2**) for a typical bike.

Table 2   COMPRESSION HISTORY

| Mileage | Compression Pressure | | |
	Left	Center	Right
New	120	125	120
2,000	120	125	120
4,000	125	125	120
6,000	125	120	115
8,000	120	90	120

Notice the sudden drop in center cylinder compression. On multicylinder machines, a 20 percent difference between compression pressures for any cylinders should be taken as an indication of trouble. Likewise, a difference of 20 percent between successive compression pressures, measured over a period of time, is also an indication of trouble. Note that a one-time compression test taken at 8,000 miles might be considered normal, but compared with

the engine's past history, it is an indication of trouble.

It is for the reasons outlined in the foregoing paragraphs that the serious motorcycle hobbyist will want to own and use his own compression gauge, and also keep a permanent record of its findings. It should be pointed out, however, that measurements taken with different gauges are not necessarily conclusive, because of production tolerances, calibration errors, and other factors.

Spark Plugs

Among the first steps to be done during any tune-up is to examine the plugs. Spark plug condition can tell much about engine condition and carburetion to a trained observer.

To remove a spark plug, first clean the area around its base to prevent dirt or other foreign material from entering the cylinder. Then unscrew the spark plug, using a 13/16 in. deep socket. If difficulty is encountered removing a spark plug, apply penetrating oil to its base and allow some 20 minutes for the oil to work in. It may also be helpful to rap the cylinder head lightly with a rubber or plastic mallet; this procedure sets up vibrations which help the penetrating oil to work in.

Figure 1 illustrates various conditions which might be encountered upon plug removal.

Normal condition—If plugs have a light tan or gray colored deposit and no abnormal gap wear or erosion, good engine, carburetion, and ignition condition are indicated. The plug in use is of the proper heat range, and may be serviced and returned to use.

Carbon fouled—Soft, dry sooty deposits are evidence of incomplete combustion and can usually be attributed to rich carburetion. This condition is also sometimes caused by weak ignition, retarded timing, or low compression. Such a plug may usually be cleaned and returned to service, but the condition which causes fouling should be corrected.

Oil fouled—This plug exhibits a black insulator tip, damp oily film over the firing end, and a carbon layer over the entire nose. Electrodes

SPARK PLUG CONDITIONS ①

NORMAL USE

OIL FOULED

CARBON FOULED

OVERHEATED

GAP BRIDGED

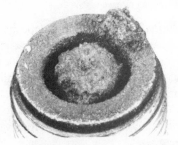

SUSTAINED PREIGNITION

WORN OUT

Photos courtesy of Champion Spark Plug Company.

will not be worn. Common causes for this condition are listed below.

    a. Oil pump misadjustment

    b. Wrong type of oil

    c. Idle speed too low

    d. Idle mixture too rich

    e. Clogged air filter

    f. Weak ignition

    g. Excessive idling

    h. Spark plug too cold

Oil fouled spark plugs may be cleaned in a pinch, but it is better to replace them. It is important to correct the cause of fouling before the engine is returned to service.

Gap bridging—Plugs with this condition exhibit gaps shorted out by combustion chamber deposits fused between electrodes. Common causes of this condition are improper fuel/oil mixture or a clogged exhaust system. Be sure to locate and correct the cause of this spark plug condition. Such plugs must be replaced with new ones.

Overheated—Overheated spark plugs exhibit burned electrodes. The insulator tip will be light gray or even chalk white. The most common cause for this condition is using a spark plug of the wrong heat range (too hot). If it is known that the correct plug is used, other causes are lean fuel mixture, engine overloading or lugging, loose carburetor mounting, or timing advanced too far. Always correct the fault before putting the bike back into service. Such plugs cannot be salvaged; replace with new ones.

Worn out—Corrosive gases formed by combustion and high voltage sparks have eroded the electrodes. Spark plugs in this condition require more voltage to fire under hard acceleration; often more than the ignition system can supply. Replace them with new plugs of the same heat range.

Preignition—If electrodes are melted, preignition is almost certainly the cause. Check for carburetor mounting or intake manifold leaks, also overadvanced ignition timing. It is also possible that a plug of the wrong heat range (too hot) is being used. Find the cause of preignition before placing the engine back into service.

Spark plugs may usually be cleaned and regapped, which will restore them to near new condition. Since the effort involved is considerable, such service may not be worth it, since new spark plugs are relatively inexpensive.

For those who wish to service used plugs, the following procedure is recommended.

1. Clean all oily deposits from the spark plug with cleaning solvent, then blow dry with compressed air. If this precaution is not taken, oily deposits will cause gumming or caking of the sandblast cleaner.

2. Place the spark plug in a sandblast cleaner and blast 3-5 seconds, then turn on air only to remove particles from the plug.

3. Repeat Step 2 as required until the plug is cleaned. Prolonged sandblasting will erode the insulator and make the plug much more susceptible to fouling.

4. Bend the side electrode up slightly, then file the center electrode so that it is no longer rounded, and the side electrode so that its edges are not rounded. The reason for this step is that less voltage is required to jump between sharp corners than between rounded edges.

5. Adjust spark plug gap to 0.028 in. (0.7mm) for all models, using a round wire gauge for measurement (**Figure 2**). A spark plug gapping tool does the best job, if one is available.

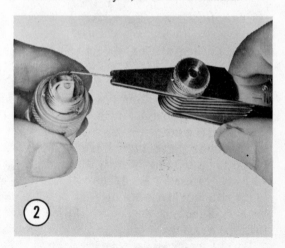

②

Carbon Removal

Two-stroke engines are particularly susceptible to carbon formation. Deposits form on the inside of the cylinder head, on top of the piston, and within the exhaust port. Combustion chamber deposits result in an increase in compression ratio, which can cause overheating, preignition, and possible severe engine damage. Carbon deposits within the exhaust port, exhaust pipe, and muffler restrict engine breathing, thus causing loss of power.

To remove carbon from the engine, it is first necessary to remove the cylinder head, cylinders, and pistons. Refer to Chapter Three for details of removing these components.

An easy method for removing cylinder head deposits is to use the rounded end of a hacksaw blade as a scraper, as shown in **Figure 3**. Be very careful not to cause any damage to the sealing surface.

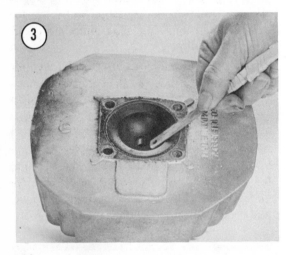

The same tool may be used for removing carbon deposits from piston heads (**Figure 4**). After cleaning all deposits from the piston head, clean all carbon and gum from piston ring grooves, using a ring groove cleaning tool or broken piston ring (**Figure 5**).

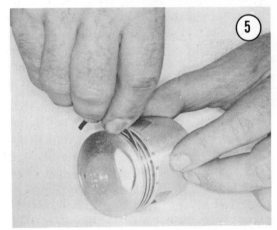

To remove piston rings, it is only necessary to spread the top ring carefully with a thumb on each end (**Figure 6**), then remove it over the top of the piston. When installing rings, be sure that the ends of the rings engage the locating pins in their grooves (**Figure 7**).

Finally, scrape all carbon deposits from each cylinder exhaust port (**Figure 8**). A blunted screwdriver is a suitable tool for this job.

Be sure to lubricate cylinders and pistons liberally before assembly. Refer to Chapter Three for details.

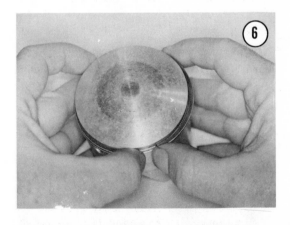

Servicing Breaker Points

Normal use of motorcycle causes the breaker points to gradually become pitted and worn. To

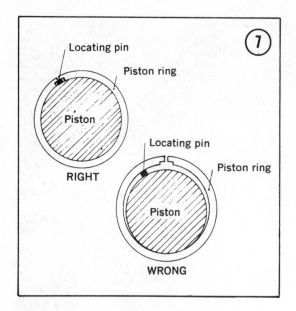

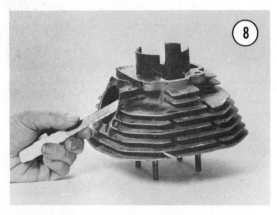

WARNING
Do not use a flammable substance such as gasoline or lacquer thinner to clean points. Excess cleaner may get trapped behind and below the breaker plate. When the engine cover is replaced, sparks from the breaker points will ignite the trapped fumes and cause an explosion.

Close the points on a piece of clean white paper such as a business card. Continue to pull the card through the closed points until no particles or discoloration remains on the card. Finally, rotate the engine and observe the points as they open and close. If they do not meet squarely, replace them (**Figure 9**).

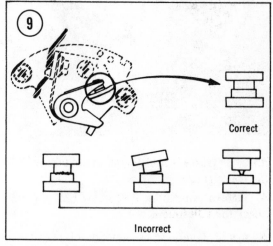

maintain peak ignition efficiency, breaker points must be serviced regularly. Do not attempt to file or dress factory Suzuki ignition points. They have a special hardened contact surface that will be destroyed if filed or sanded. Pitted points must be replaced.

Oil or dirt may get on the points, resulting in premature failure. Common causes for this condition are defective crankshaft seals, improper breaker cam lubrication, or lack of care when the crankcase cover is removed.

If point springs are weak, breaker points will bounce and cause misfiring at high speeds.

Clean and regap breaker points every 2,000 miles (3,000 km). To clean the points, spray with a non-flammable contact cleaner available at most auto parts stores or motorcycle shops.

After the points have been dressed and cleaned, they must be adjusted. See **Figure 10**.

1. Rotate the engine until the points for the center cylinder are open to their widest distance apart. Marks (C), (L), and (R) by each set of points identify points for center, left, and right cylinders.

2. Loosen the center breaker point attaching screw (A) slightly, so that the stationary point may be moved with a screwdriver in pry slots (B).

3. Insert a clean 0.014 in. (0.35mm) feeler gauge into the opening between the points. Move the stationary point so that there is barely perceptible drag on the feeler gauge as it is pulled out from between the points. Be sure that

no oil or grease is transferred to the points from the feeler gauge.

4. Tighten point attaching screw (A), then recheck the adjustment.

5. Apply a very small amount of distributor cam lubricant to the felt lubricator. A bead the size of a small match head is more than enough.

6. Repeat Steps 1 through 5 for the remaining cylinders.

7. Ignition timing is affected by any change in point gap. Always adjust timing after servicing breaker points.

Replacing Breaker Points

Suzuki machines are equipped with either Kokusan or Denso ignition systems. Although entire breaker assemblies are interchangeable, individual parts, such as breaker points, are not. Therefore, it is necessary to identify the system on the motorcycle in question. **Figures 11 and 12** illustrate Kokusan and Denso systems, respectively. Be sure to specify which type of

system is installed when ordering ignition system components.

To remove and replace breaker points in either system, proceed as follows.

1. Remove the breaker point attaching screw.

2. Remove both wires from the points.

3. Clean the breaker cam thoroughly, then apply a very small quantity of breaker cam lubricant.

4. Reverse the removal procedure to install new breaker points.

5. Be sure to adjust point gap and ignition timing.

Certain special precautions must be taken on model GT380, since the breaker cam is driven by a nylon gear (**Figure 13**). Should it become necessary to loosen the breaker cam nut, be sure to remove the right crankcase cover first. Failure to do so will probably result in a broken gear. Two crankcase cover screws are under the contact breaker plate, so the breaker plate must be removed first. It is not necessary to remove the

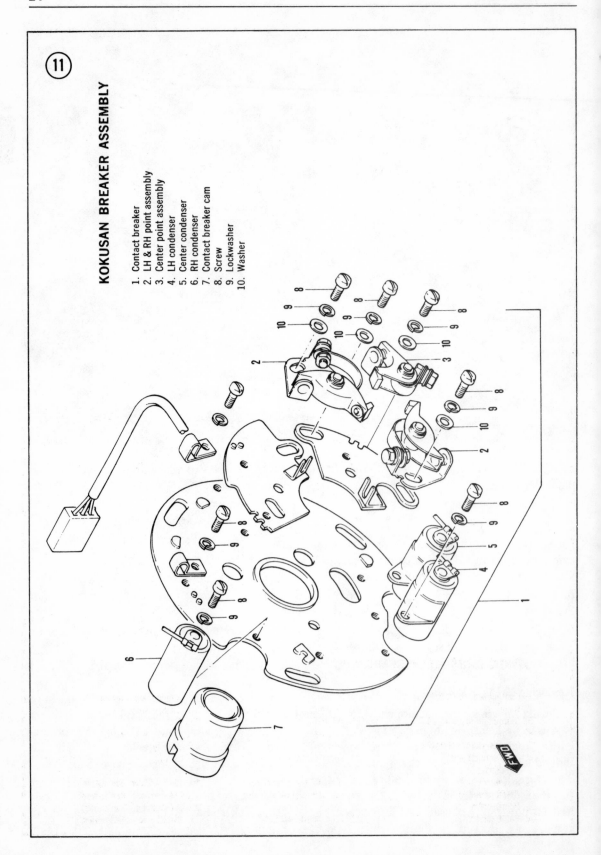

⑪

KOKUSAN BREAKER ASSEMBLY

1. Contact breaker
2. LH & RH point assembly
3. Center point assembly
4. LH condenser
5. Center condenser
6. RH condenser
7. Contact breaker cam
8. Screw
9. Lockwasher
10. Washer

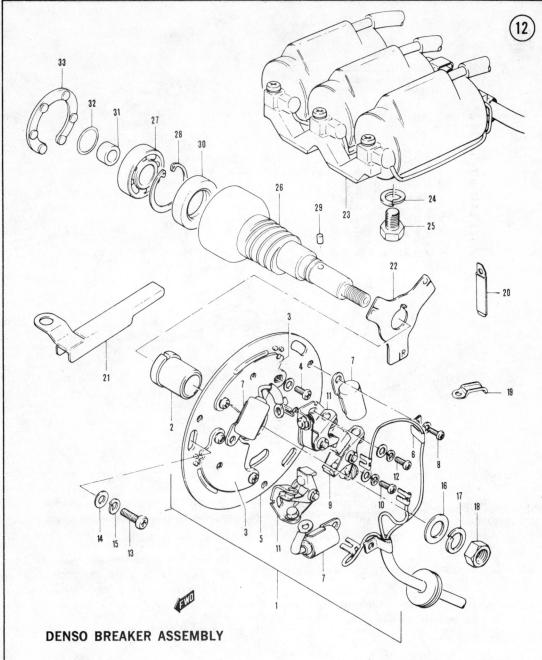

DENSO BREAKER ASSEMBLY

1. Contact breaker assembly
2. Cam
3. Contact point shift plate
4. Screw
5. Breaker stator assembly
6. Lead wire clamp
7. Condenser
8. Screw
9. Point assembly
10. Point screw
11. Point assembly

12. Screw
13. Screw
14. Washer
15. Lockwasher
16. Washer
17. Lockwasher
18. Nut
19. Breaker lead wire clamp
20. Breaker lead wire clamp
21. Lead wire plate
22. Ignition timing plate

23. Ignition coil assembly
24. Lockwasher
25. Bolt
26. Breaker cam shaft
27. Bearing
28. Circlip
29. Pin
30. Breaker cam shaft oil seal
31. Breaker cam shaft spacer
32. Breaker cam shaft O-ring
33. Breaker cam shaft rubber

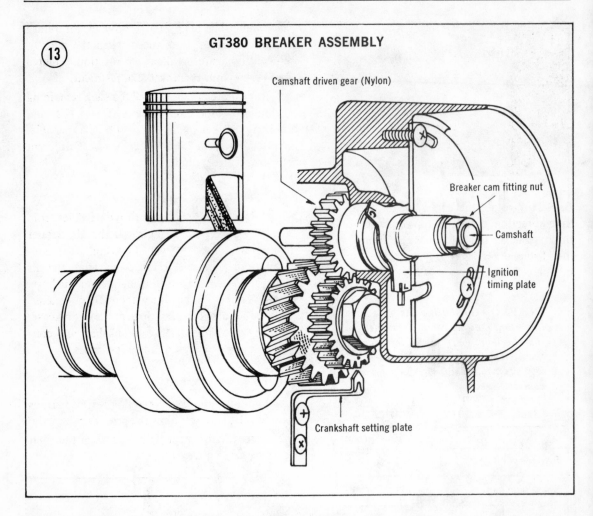

GT380 BREAKER ASSEMBLY

⑬

Camshaft driven gear (Nylon)

Breaker cam fitting nut

Camshaft

Ignition timing plate

Crankshaft setting plate

breaker cam and timing plate before crankcase cover removal.

To reinstall the right crankcase cover, proceed as follows. If these steps are not followed exactly, it will not be possible to set ignition timing.

1. Align the punched mark on the breaker cam shaft drive gear with the alignment mark on the crankshaft setting plate.

2. Align the red line by the (L) timing mark on the timing plate with the alignment mark on the right crankcase cover.

3. Be sure the alignment pin on the crankcase matches the hole on the crankcase cover.

Ignition Timing

Any change in point gap, including that which results from normal wear of breaker point sur-

faces and rubbing blocks, affects ignition timing. To adjust timing on these models, proceed as follows.

> NOTE: *It is important that left cylinder timing be adjusted first, because any adjustment to it affects both other cylinders also.*

1. Insert a dial gauge into the left cylinder spark plug hole (**Figure 14**).

2. Slowly rotate the engine in its normal running direction until the left piston is at top dead center, as determined by the dial gauge.

3. Set the dial indicator to zero.

4. Rotate the engine in reverse to lower the piston about ¼ in. (6mm).

5. Connect a test lamp, buzzer, or other continuity tester across the points for the left cylinder.

6. Slowly rotate the engine in its normal running direction until the timing tester or continuity checker indicates that the points open at the distance below top dead center specified in **Table 3**.

NOTE: *On GT380 models, it is very important that the engine be turned by the alternator bolt on the left side of the engine. This procedure ensures that any slack that exists between breaker cam drive gears is taken up.*

Table 3   IGNITION SPECIFICATIONS

	in.	(mm)
Breaker point gap	0.014	(0.35)
Spark plug gap	0.028	(0.7)
Ignition timing (distance BTDC)		
GT380 J, K	0.117	(2.99)*
	0.115	(2.93)**
GT380 L	0.094	(2.40)
GT380 M	0.090	(2.30)*
	0.088	(2.25)**
GT380 A, B	0.082	(2.09)*
	0.080	(2.05)**
GT550	0.132	(3.37)
GT750 J, K, L, M	0.143	(3.64)*
	0.134	(3.42)**
GT750 A, B	0.142	(3.63)*
	0.134	(3.42)**

* Right and left cylinders   ** Center cylinder

7. If the points do not open at the specified distance, refer to **Figure 15**. Slightly loosen timing plate screws (A), then move breaker contact mounting plate (B) to advance or retard timing. Timing is advanced when the plate is moved opposite breaker cam rotation. Tighten the screws and recheck the adjustment.

8. Repeat Steps 1 through 7 for each remaining cylinder, by loosening screws (D) or (E), and moving breaker plates (F) or (G) as applicable. Note that on GT750 models, timing is different for the center cylinder.

Air Cleaner

The air cleaner filters abrasive particles from air on its way to the engine. If the air cleaner becomes clogged, power drops and fuel consumption increases. Remove dirt from the air cleaner by brushing or blowing with an air hose.

Never operate the bike without an air cleaner. Since fuel and air pass through the crankcase, dirt drawn in may damage crankshaft and connecting rod bearings in only a few miles.

Oil Pump Adjustment

Oil pump adjustment is similar for the various models. Be sure to follow the procedure exactly.

1. Remove alignment hole plug from the right carburetor (**Figure 16**).

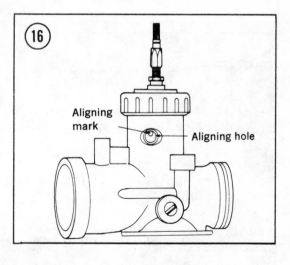

Aligning mark

Aligning hole

2. Remove oil pump cover.

3. Turn throttle grip until mark on throttle slide is at the top of the hole.

4. Loosen pump cable adjuster locknut, then turn cable adjuster until the line on the oil pump aligns with mark (**Figure 17**) on the oil pump.

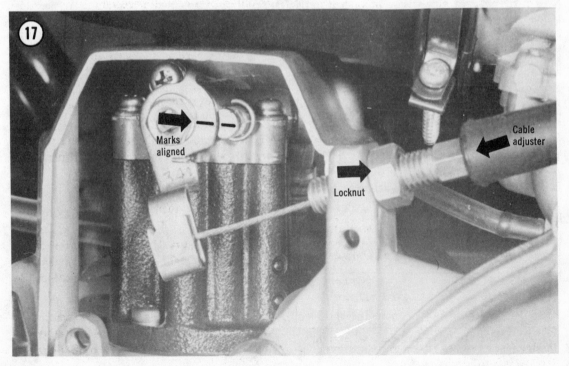

5. Release the throttle, tighten pump cable lock-nut, then recheck adjustment.

6. Replace alignment hole cover screw.

VM Carburetor Adjustment

Begin carburetor adjustment by turning in each idle mixture screw until it seats lightly, then turn it out the number of turns specified in **Table 4**. At higher altitudes, above approximately 3,000 feet (1,000 meters), back out each screw an additional turn.

Table 4   IDLE MIXTURE ADJUSTMENT

Model	Turns
GT380	1¼
GT550 J, K	1¼
GT550 (all others)	1½
GT750 J, K	1½
GT750 L	¼
GT750 M, A, B	¾

NOTE: Tolerance for adjustments is ± ¼ turn.
Adjust for smoothest idle.

Turn each throttle cable adjuster to provide 0.1-0.2 in. (3-5mm) play in each throttle cable. There is an adjuster at the top of each carburetor.

The simplest method for adjusting each carburetor idle speed screw is to start the engine, warm it for a few minutes, then stop it and disconnect all but one spark plug lead. Restart the engine, then very slowly reduce idle speed by turning the idle speed screw until the engine just dies. Repeat this procedure with each remaining cylinder. Reconnect the spark plug leads, then screw equally to achieve the idle speed specified in **Table 5**.

Table 5   IDLE SPEED SCREW ADJUSTMENT

Model	Idle Speed
GT350	1,100 rpm
GT550	1,100 rpm
GT750	1,000 rpm

NOTE: Spark plugs in nonfiring cylinders may become fouled during this procedure. Clean them if this situation occurs.

Carburetor Synchronization

Power output will be unbalanced unless all cylinders are synchronized. If one cylinder receives more fuel/air mixture from its associated carburetor than the other cylinders, overall poor performance will result. To synchronize the carburetors, proceed as follows.

1. Remove the screw from the alignment hole in each carburetor.

2. Open the throttle approximately halfway, until the alignment mark (**Figure 18**) one one cylinder is even with the top edge of the inspection hole. Hold the throttle grip in this position.

3. Turn the cable adjusters on the 2 remaining carburetors so that the alignment marks occupy the same relative position as that of the reference carburetor.

4. Return the throttle to idle position. Be sure that there is at least 0.04 in. (1mm) play in the throttle cable at each carburetor.

5. Install each alignment hole cover screw.

6. Finally, adjust throttle cable play at the throttle grip. Turn the adjuster to provide 0.04-0.08 in. (1-2mm) slack in the cable, measured at the throttle grip. This adjustment may affect oil pump adjustment, so be sure to readjust the oil pump lever cable if necessary.

BS 40 Carburetor Adjustment

If the carburetor has been disassembled, as after overhaul, perform Steps 1 through 15. If just routine adjustment is required, as during engine tune-up, perform Steps 4 through 15.

1. Turn throttle valve adjustment screw (1, **Figure 19**) until throttle butterfly valve (2, **Figure 20**) aligns with edge of No. 1 bypass hole (1, Figure 20).

2. Gently turn each idle mixture screw until it bottoms lightly, then back it out as specified in Table 4.

3. Refer to **Figure 21**. Turn cable adjuster (1) to provide about 0.1-0.2 in. (2-3mm) side play under light finger pressure to throttle cables. Be sure to tighten all locknuts.

4. Start engine and warm it thoroughly.

5. Turn throttle valve stop screw (1, **Figure 22**) until engine runs at approximately 3,000 rpm.

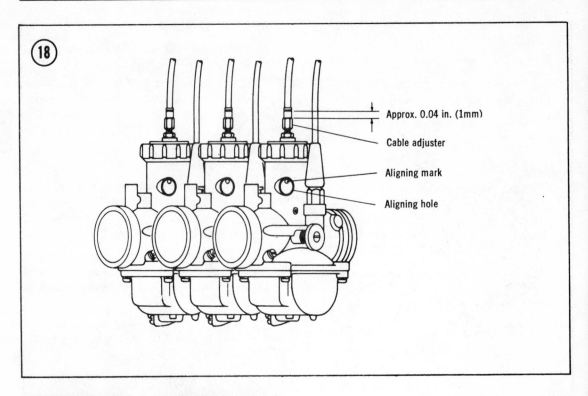

Approx. 0.04 in. (1mm)

Cable adjuster

Aligning mark

Aligning hole

1. Throttle valve adjustment screw   2. Throttle valve lever

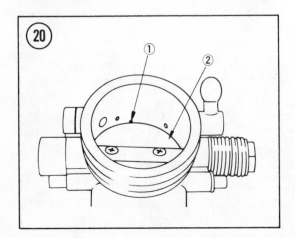

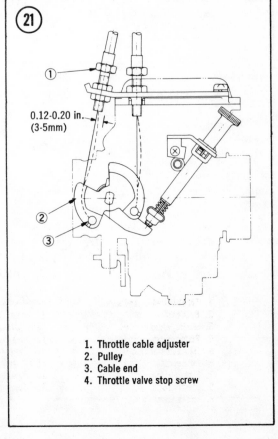

0.12-0.20 in. (3-5mm)

1. Throttle cable adjuster
2. Pulley
3. Cable end
4. Throttle valve stop screw

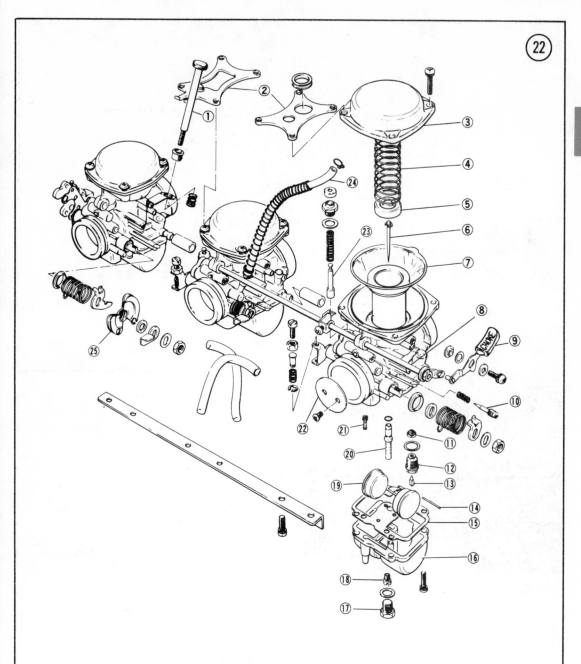

BS CARBURETOR

1. Throttle valve stop screw
2. Bracket
3. Mixing chamber top
4. Piston valve spring
5. Jet needle set plate
6. Jet needle
7. Piston valve
8. Starter rod
9. Choke lever

10. Pilot screw
11. Fuel strainer
12. Valve seat
13. Needle valve
14. Float arm pin
15. Float chamber gasket
16. Float chamber
17. Drain plug

18. Main jet
19. Float
20. Needle jet
21. Pilot jet
22. Throttle valve
23. Starter plunger
24. Fuel hose
25. Pulley

Do not confuse this screw with individual screws on carburetors.

> NOTE: *It is necessary to initially set idle at approximately 3,000 rpm to enable engine to run on only one cylinder for the remainder of the adjustment procedure.*

6. Stop engine and remove left and center spark plug wires.

7. Start engine and adjust throttle valve stop screw on right cylinder (4, Figure 21) until engine idles at 1,000 rpm.

8. Stop engine and disconnect right spark plug wire. Connect center spark plug wire.

9. Start engine and adjust throttle valve adjustment screw (1, Figure 19) on center carburetor until engine idles at 1,000 rpm.

10. Stop engine and disconnect center spark plug wire. Connect left spark plug wire.

11. Start engine and adjust throttle valve adjustment screw (1, Figure 19) on left carburetor until engine idles at 1,000 rpm.

12. Stop engine and connect right and center spark plug wires.

13. Start engine. Engine speed will be approximately 3,000-4,000 rpm.

14. Turn throttle valve stop screw (4, Figure 21) until engine idles at 1,000 rpm.

15. Check oil pump adjustment and readjust if necessary.

Battery Service

Tune-up time is also battery service time. Complete battery service information is contained in Chapter Five. Briefly, the following items should be attend to regularly.

1. Test state of charge. Recharge if at half charge (1.220 specific gravity) or less.

2. Add distilled water if required.

3. Clean battery top.

4. Clean and tighten terminals.

Drive Chain

Inspect the drive chain periodically. Pay particular attention to rollers and link plates. Replace the chain if there is any doubt about its condition. Adjust chain play to 0.6-0.8 in. (15-20mm).

Refer to Chapter Seven for further details on drive chain service.

Electrical Equipment

Check all electrical equipment. Refer to Chapter Five for electrical system service.

Fuel Strainer

Remove and clean the fuel strainer element. Be sure that the fuel petcock does not leak. Dirty fuel strainers are a major cause of carburetor flooding.

Other Service Items

Go over the entire bike carefully, examining it for loose spokes, bent wheels, oil leaks, or anything else which could result in unsafe riding conditions or cause major problems later. Correct any such condition at once.

CHAPTER THREE

ENGINE, TRANSMISSION, AND CLUTCH

This chapter describes removal, disassembly, service, and reassembly of the engine, transmission, and clutch. It is suggested that the engine be serviced without removing it from the chassis except for overhaul of the crankshaft assembly, transmission, gearshift mechanism, or bearings. Operating principles of two-stroke engines are also discussed in this chapter.

ENGINE PRINCIPLES

Figures 1 through 4 illustrate operation of the two-stroke engine. During this discussion, assume that the crankshaft is rotating counterclockwise. In **Figure 1**, as the piston travels downward, a scavenging port (A) between the crankcase and the cylinder is uncovered. The exhaust gases, which are under pressure, leave the cylinder through the exhaust port (B), which is also opened by the downward movement of the piston. A fresh fuel/air charge, which has previously been compressed slightly, travels from the crankcase (C) to the cylinder through the scavenging port (A) as the port opens. Since the incoming charge is under pressure, it rushes into the cylinder quickly and helps to expel the exhaust gases from the previous cycle.

Figure 2 illustrates the next phase of the cycle. As the crankshaft continues to rotate, the piston

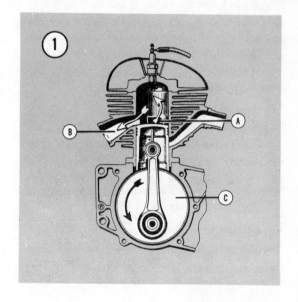

moves upward, closing the exhaust and scavenging ports. As the piston continues upward, the air/fuel mixture in the cylinder is compressed. Notice also that a low pressure area is created in the crankcase at the same time. Further upward movement of the piston uncovers the intake port (D). A fresh fuel/air charge is then drawn into the crankcase through the intake port because of the low pressure created by the upward piston movement.

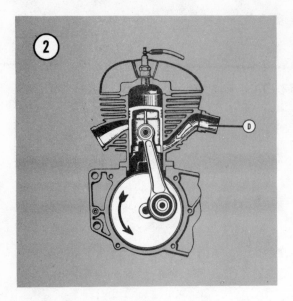

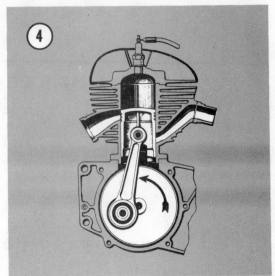

The third phase is shown in **Figure 3**. As the piston approaches top dead center, the spark plug fires, igniting the compressed mixture. The piston is then driven downward by the expanding gases.

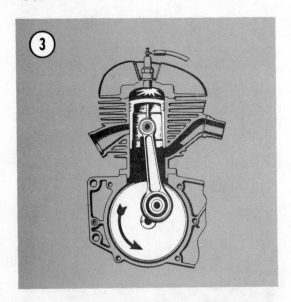

When the top of the piston uncovers the exhaust port, the fourth phase begins, as shown in **Figure 4**. The exhaust gases leave the cylinder through the exhaust port. As the piston continues downward, the intake port is closed and the mixture in the crankcase is compressed in preparation for the next cycle.

It can be seen from the foregoing discussion that every downward stroke of the piston is a power stroke. Three-cylinder engines are so arranged that one cylinder fires for each 120 degrees rotation of the crankshaft, thus producing three power strokes for each crankshaft revolution.

ENGINE LUBRICATION

A conventional two-stroke engine cannot receive its lubrication from an oil supply in the crankcase. Oil splash in the crankcase would be carried into the cylinders with the fuel/air charge, resulting in high oil consumption and spark plug fouling. To overcome this objection, Suzuki three-cylinder engines utilize an engine-driven oil pump to deliver lubricating oil under pressure to the crankshaft bearings and to the lower connecting rod bearings and cylinder walls. The output from the pump is controlled not only by engine speed, but also by throttle position, which is closely related to engine load. Therefore, the engine is supplied with the proper amount of oil under all operating conditions. **Figure 5** illustrates a typical oil distribution system.

A further refinement is Suzuki Recycle Injection System (SRIS). See **Figure 6**. The purpose of this system is to reduce exhaust smoke.

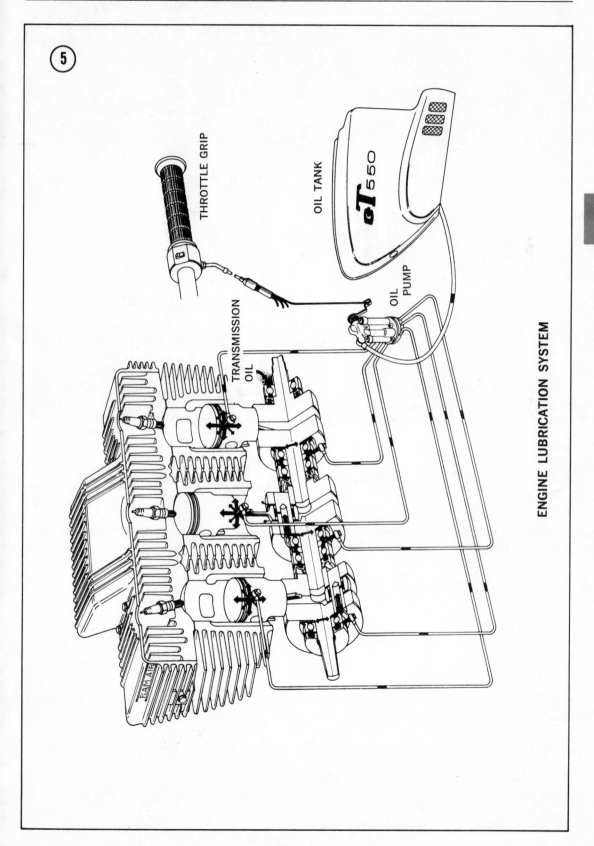

5

THROTTLE GRIP

OIL TANK

GT550

OIL PUMP

TRANSMISSION OIL

RAM AIR

ENGINE LUBRICATION SYSTEM

3

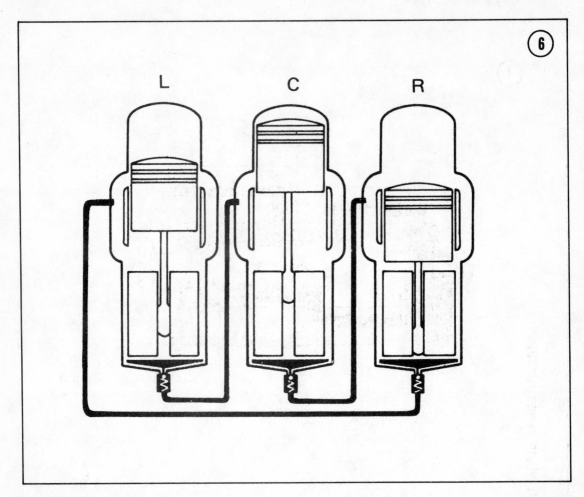

Small quantities of oil accumulate in each crank chamber during normal use of the motorcycle. Positive pressure in each crank chamber forces any accumulated oil through a check valve into the induction tract of another cylinder.

OIL PUMP

Figure 7 (next page) illustrates a typical oil pump. The pump is driven by gears, so that it operates at all times when the engine is running. Never attempt to disassemble the oil pump. Replace the pump in the event of any malfunction.

Oil Pump Adjustment

Oil pump adjustment is similar for the various models. Be sure to follow the procedure exactly.

1. Remove the aligning hole plug from the right carburetor (**Figure 8**).

2. Turn the throttle grip until the mark on the throttle slide is at the top of the hole (**Figure 9**).

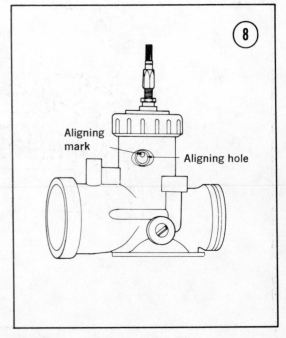

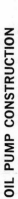

OIL PUMP CONSTRUCTION

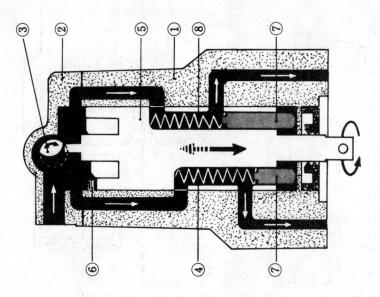

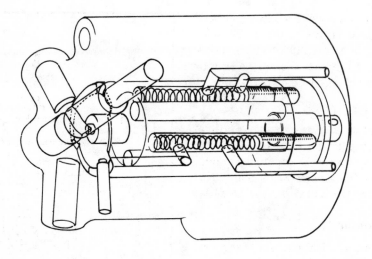

1. Oil pump body
2. Pump control body
3. Control cam
4. Plunger hole

5. Pump valve
6. Cam guide
7. Plunger
8. Spring

3. Remove oil pump cover, and loosen the pump cable adjuster lock nut. Turn the cable adjuster until the line on the oil pump lever aligns with the mark (**Figure 10**) on oil pump.

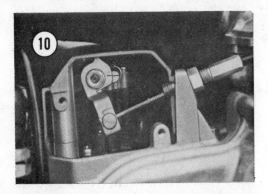

4. Release the throttle, tighten the pump cable lock nut, then recheck the adjustment.

5. Replace the alignment hole cover screw.

Bleeding the Oil Pump

Air enters the oil pump and lines whenever the pump is disconnected or the tank has run dry. After such an occurrence, the oil pump must be bled.

To bleed air from the inlet side, loosen the bleeder screw (**Figure 11**), until oil flows freely, with no air bubbles. Then tighten the screw.

After the inlet line is bled, start the engine and run it at 1,500 to 2,000 rpm. Hold the pump control lever in the full open position by hand, until all air is bled from the outlet tubes. If any bubbles longer than 0.4 inch (10 millimeters) appear, stop the engine, then force a small amount of oil into the outlet tubes at the check valves, as shown in **Figure 12**. Check the connections at inlet and discharge ports, the vinyl tubes, and plunger housing. If the bubbles disappear when oil or grease is applied to these points, air leakage is occurring.

Check Valves

Check valves prevent oil from flowing back into the pump as a result of pressure in the

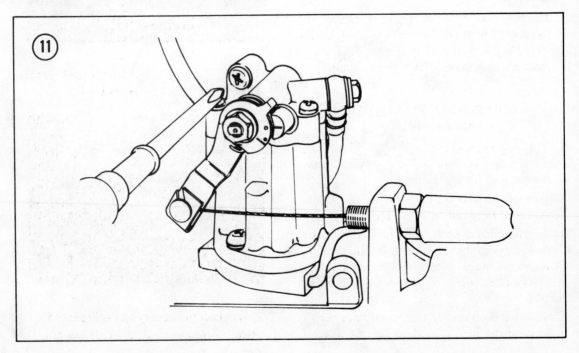

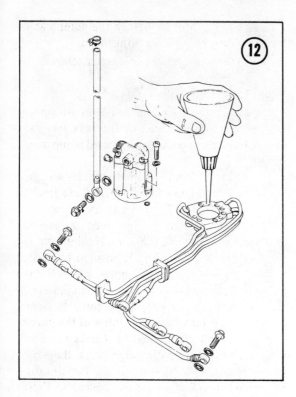

crankcase. Pour about 0.3 ounce (10 cubic centimeters) of oil into the check valve mounting hole before you install the check valve. Do not attempt to disassemble the check valves.

Engine Oil

Do not mix brands or types of engine oil. Select a good brand of 2-cycle oil and stick with it. Some types, particularly synthetics, are not compatible with those having a mineral oil base.

PREPARATION FOR ENGINE DISASSEMBLY

1. Thoroughly clean the engine exterior of dirt, oil, and foreign material, using one of the cleaners formulated for the purpose.

2. Be sure you have the proper tools for the job. See *General Information* in Chapter One.

3. As you remove parts from the engine, place them in trays in the order of their disassembly. Doing so will make reassembly faster and easier, and will ensure correct installation of all engine parts.

4. Note that disassembly procedures vary slightly between the various models. Be sure to read the steps carefully and follow those which apply to your engine.

ENGINE REMOVAL

The procedure for removing the engine is generally similar for all models. The following steps are set forth as a guide:

Models GT380 and GT550

1. If the engine runs, start it and allow it to run for a few minutes to warm the transmission oil. Then stop the engine and drain the oil.

2. Turn the fuel petcock to OFF. On models with automatic fuel cocks, turn the lever to ON.

3. Disconnect the fuel line from the fuel cock. If the machine has an automatic fuel cock, disconnect all lines (**Figure 13**) from the fuel cock.

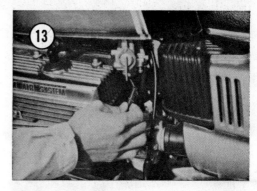

4. Remove the rubber fuel tank retaining strap, then lift off the fuel tank (**Figure 14**).

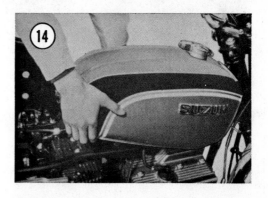

5. Disconnect the battery leads (**Figure 15**).

6. Remove all spark plug wires (**Figure 16**).

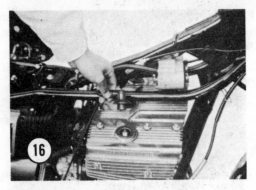

7. Disconnect the wiring to the breaker contacts (**Figure 17**).

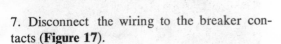

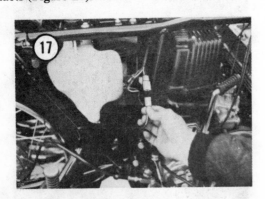

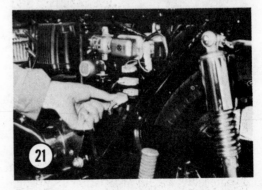

8. Remove rear stop light switch (**Figure 18**).

9. Disconnect the tachometer cable (**Figure 19**).

10. Disconnect the starter cable at terminal "M" at the starter relay (**Figure 20**).

11. Disconnect alternator wiring (**Figure 21**).

12. Disconnect the oil pump control cable (**Figure 22**). **Figure 23** illustrates the procedure for releasing the pump wire.

13. Remove oil line at the oil tank (**Figure 24**). Be sure to plug the oil tank outlet to prevent loss of oil. A tire valve cap is a suitable plug.

14. Loosen the right footrest and rear brake lever, then remove the brake pedal (**Figure 25**).

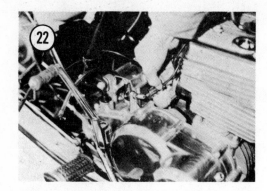

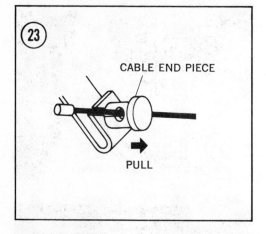

CABLE END PIECE

→ PULL

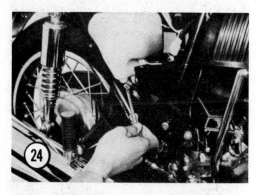

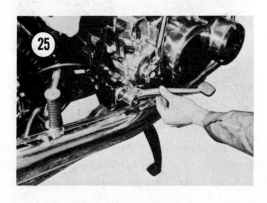

15. Remove the air cleaner (**Figure 26**).

16. Remove all three carburetors (**Figure 27**).

17. Remove the gearshift pedal (**Figure 28**).

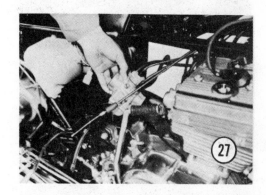

18. Remove the left footrest (**Figure 29**).

19. Remove clutch release cover (**Figure 30**).

20. Remove engine sprocket cover (**Figure 31**).

21. Remove three bolts, then rotate engine sprocket retainer slightly and remove it from the output shaft (**Figure 32**).

22. Remove the engine sprocket (**Figure 33**).

23. Remove both of the cylinder head covers (**Figure 34**).

24. Remove both rear footrests (**Figure 35**).

25. Remove both outer mufflers and exhaust pipes (**Figure 36**).

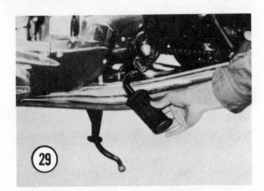

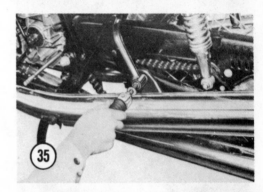

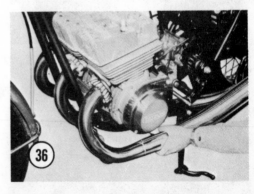

26. Loosen two connectors (**Figure 37**), then pull both center mufflers backwards.

27. Remove the center exhaust pipe (**Figure 38**).

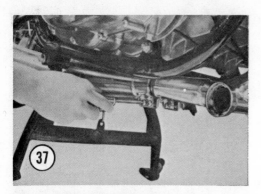

28. Remove the four engine mount bolts (**Figure 39**) on model GT550, or the three bolts (**Figure 40**) on model GT380.

29. Remove engine mounting plate (**Figure 41**).

30. Make a final check of the engine for any attachments which might have been missed.

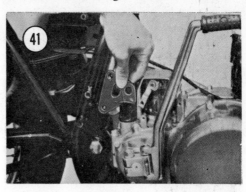

31. Straddle the motorcycle, then lift the engine and pull it out from the right side of the frame (**Figure 42**).

Model GT750

Engine removal is generally similar to that described in the foregoing steps, with the following additions:

1. Drain the cooling system by removing the drain plug (1), shown in **Figure 43**.

2. Disconnect the radiator inlet hose (see **Figure 44**).

3. Remove the fan, together with its bracket (**Figure 45**).

CYLINDER HEAD

The cylinder head may be removed for service without removing the engine. On model GT750, the cooling system must be drained.

1. Water drain plug

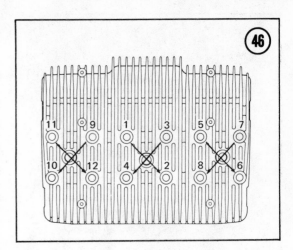

GT550. Loosening and tightening sequence for model GT750 are shown in **Figure 47**.

To install the cylinder head, run the nuts down until they are snug, then tighten them in the same order as they were loosened. Always use a new gasket. Torque the nuts as in **Table 1**.

Table 1   CYLINDER HEAD NUT TORQUES

| Model | Torque | |
	Pound-Feet	Kilogram-centimeters
GT380	26	350
GT550	18-29	250-400
GT750 (8mm)	13-16	180-220
(10mm)	22-29	300-400

Removing Carbon Deposits

Carbon deposits in the combustion chamber result in an increase in compression ratio and can cause preignition, overheating, and excessive fuel consumption. To remove these deposits, scrape them off with the rounded end of a hacksaw blade or a screwdriver. Be careful that you don't damage the gasket surface.

Checking Warpage

The cylinder head is subjected to vibration, pressure, and high temperature. These conditions may result in warpage. To check for this condition, lay a straightedge along the cylinder head at each location shown in **Figure 48**. Measure clearance between the straightedge and cylinder head with a feeler gauge. Repair or replace the

Removal and Installation

Wait until the engine is cool before removing the cylinder head to avoid possible warpage. Then loosen and remove the cylinder head nuts in proper sequence. **Figure 46** shows loosening and tightening sequence for models GT380 and

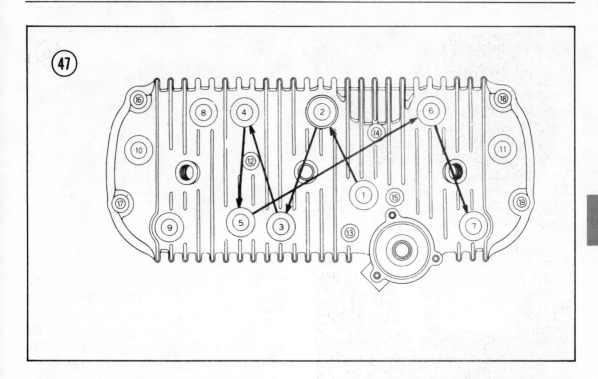

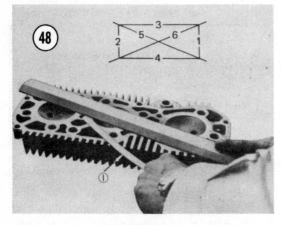

1. Feeler gauge

CYLINDERS

Cylinders are made of aluminum alloy. On models GT380 and GT550, they are mounted individually. Cylinders on model GT750 are combined into one casting. After wear from long usage or damage from piston seizure, the cylinders may be bored and honed.

Cylinder Removal

Remove and tag each SRIS tube. Remove the cylinder retaining nuts (**Figure 49**). Tap the cylinder around the exhaust ports with a plastic mallet, then pull it away from the crankcase.

cylinder head if that portion of the cylinder head that covers any one cylinder is warped more than 0.012 inch (0.03 millimeter), or if warp exceeds 0.06 inch (0.15 millimeter) for the whole unit.

If warpage is found, it may be possible to salvage the cylinder head. Fasten a sheet of No. 200 emery paper to a surface plate, then move the head back and forth until the gasket surface is no longer warped. Finish the job with No. 400 emery paper. Do not take off any more metal than is necessary. Clean the cylinder head carefully after you finish.

Stuff clean rags into the crankcase openings to prevent entry of any foreign material.

Checking the Cylinders

Measure cylinder wall wear at the locations shown in **Figure 50** with a cylinder gauge or inside micrometer, as shown in **Figure 51**. Position the instrument parallel and then at right angles to the crankshaft at each measurement depth. If the difference between any 2 measurements exceeds the service limit (**Table 2**), replace or rebore the cylinder. Oversize pistons are available.

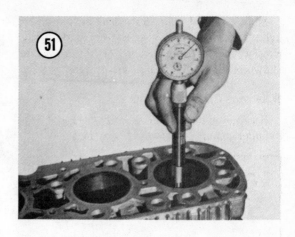

Table 2   CYLINDER SERVICE LIMITS

| Model | Service Limit | |
	Inch	(Millimeter)
GT380	0.0039	(0.10)
GT550	0.0039	(0.10)
GT750	0.0018	(0.07)

If the cylinder is to be rebored, first add the desired oversize to the standard cylinder bore. The total will be the diameter to which the cylinder should be bored and honed. After boring and honing, the difference between maximum and minimum diameters should not be more than 0.0004 inch (0.01 millimeter).

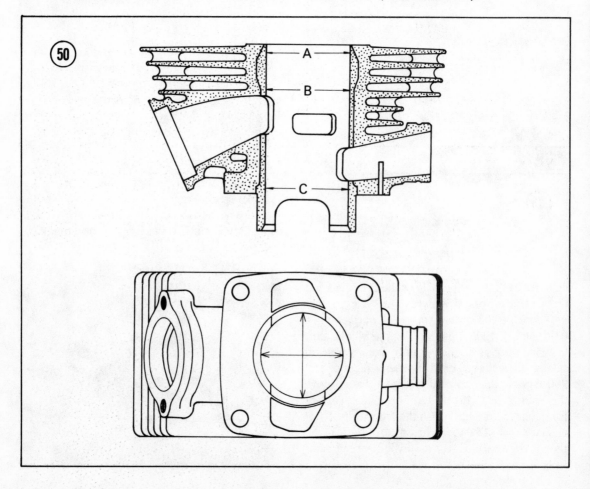

It is essential that the sharp edges of the cylinder parts be broken to prevent rapid piston ring wear and noise. Chamfer the edges as shown in **Figure 52**, using a file or hand grinder.

Removing Carbon Deposits

Scrape the carbon deposits from around the cylinder exhaust port, as shown in **Figure 53**.

The rounded end of a hacksaw blade is a suitable tool for carbon removal.

Cylinder Installation

Be sure that each piston ring end gap is aligned with the locating pin in the ring groove. Lubricate the piston and cylinder, then insert the piston into the lower end of the cylinder. It

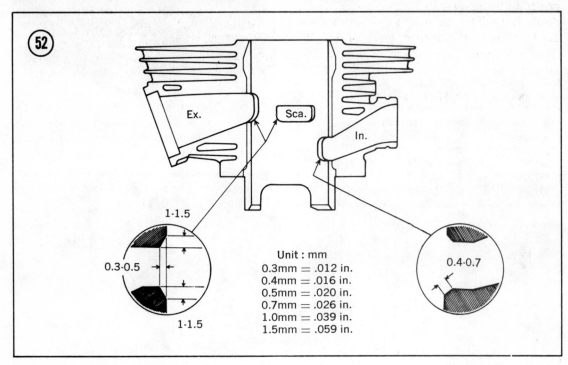

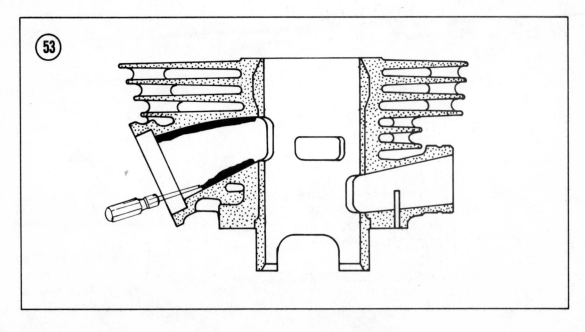

will be necessary to compress each piston ring as it goes into the cylinder. Always use a new cylinder base gasket upon reassembly. Use no sealer on the cylinder base gasket.

PISTON PIN, PISTON, AND PISTON RINGS

Piston Pin

Remove the clips at each end of the piston pin (**Figure 54**). Then press out the piston pin. It is easier to press out piston pins if the pistons are first heated by wrapping them in rags which have been soaked in hot water.

Examine the piston pin for scratches or wear. To check the bearing for wear, insert the bearing into the small end of a new connecting rod, then insert a new piston pin into the bearing. Replace the bearing if radial clearance is excessive. Typical standard clearances are 0.00012 to 0.00086 inch (0.003 to 0.022 millimeter). Any clearance over 0.0018 inch (0.045 millimeter) should be considered excessive.

Piston

Scrape the carbon from the head of the piston (**Figure 55**). Then clean all carbon and gum from the piston ring grooves using a broken piston ring, or a ring groove cleaning tool. Any deposits left in the grooves will cause the rings to stick, thereby causing gas blowby and loss of power.

A piston showing signs of seizure will result in noise, loss of power, and damage to the cylinder wall. If such a piston is reused without cor-

rection, another seizure will develop. To correct this condition, lightly smooth the affected area with No. 40 emery paper or a fine oilstone

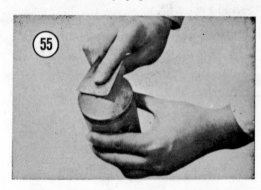

(**Figure 56**). Replace the piston if it is deeply scratched.

Piston clearance is the difference between the maximum piston diameter and the minimum cylinder diameter. Measure the outside diameter of the piston skirt (**Figure 57**) at right angles to the piston pin. **Table 3** specifies the distance from the bottom of the piston skirt (**Figure 58**) at which the measurement should be made.

Table 3   PISTON CLEARANCE

Model	Distance	
	Inch	(Millimeter)
GT380	1.02	(26)
GT550	1.14	(29)
GT750	1.26	(32)

Install the piston with the arrow mark (**Figure 59**) pointing toward the front of the machine. This is important because the hole for the piston is offset slightly to prevent piston slap.

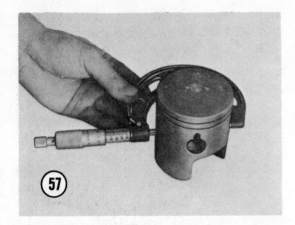

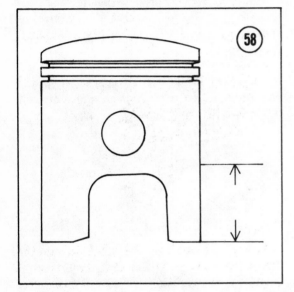

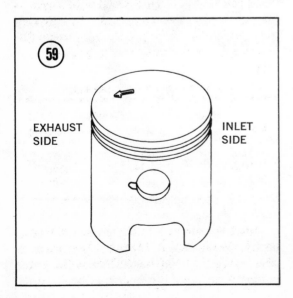

Piston Rings

Suzuki three-cylinder machines are equipped with keystone pistons and rings. A sectional view of a keystone ring is shown in **Figure 60**. The design of the keystone ring uses combustion gas pressure to force the ring outward against the cylinder wall.

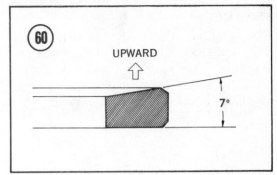

An important advantage of the keystone ring is illustrated in **Figure 61**. As the piston moves up and down, the piston ring moves inward and outward, thus varying ring groove clearance. This varying clearance tends to prevent the ring from sticking in its groove.

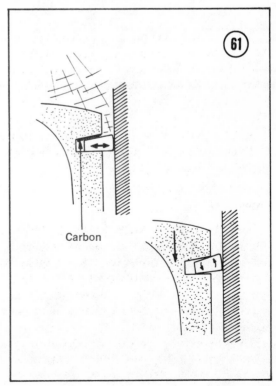

To remove the piston rings, spread the top ring with a thumb on each end, as shown in **Figure 62**, then remove the ring from the top. Repeat this procedure for the remaining ring. Be careful so that you don't break or damage the rings, or damage the piston.

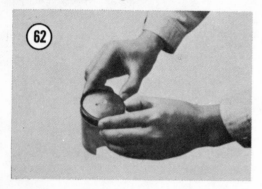

Measure each ring for wear as shown in **Figures 63 and 64**. Insert the ring approximately 0.2 inch (5 millimeters) into the cylinder, then measure the gap with a feeler gauge. To ensure that the ring is inserted squarely into the cylinder, push it into position with the head of the piston. If either ring gap exceeds the wear limit (**Table 4**), replace both rings.

Table 4   RING GAP

Wear Limit Model	Inch	(Millimeter)	Standard Ring Gap Inch	(Millimeter)
GT380	0.006-0.014	(0.15-0.35)	0.039	(1.0)
GT550	0.006-0.014	(0.15-0.35)	0.039	(1.0)
GT750	0.006-0.014	(0.15-0.35)	0.027	(0.7)

When you replace the rings, first install the lower one, then the upper one. Use a pair of piston ring pliers, if available. If not, spread the

rings carefully with your thumbs, just enough to slip them over the piston. Align the end gaps with the locating pin in each ring groove, as shown in Figure 62. Be sure that any markings are upward.

Measure ring groove side clearance, using a feeler gauge (**Figure 65**). Replace the piston and/or the piston ring if side clearance exceeds 0.006 inch (0.15 millimeter).

CLUTCH

All models are equipped with wet multidisc clutches. A handlebar lever controls the clutch.

Clutch Operation

Figure 66 is a sectional view of a typical clutch assembly, showing alternating cork and steel plates. The cork plates are splined to the engine shaft and always rotate with the shaft. When the hand lever is released, clutch springs press the steel and cork plates together, thereby transmitting engine torque to the transmission. As the

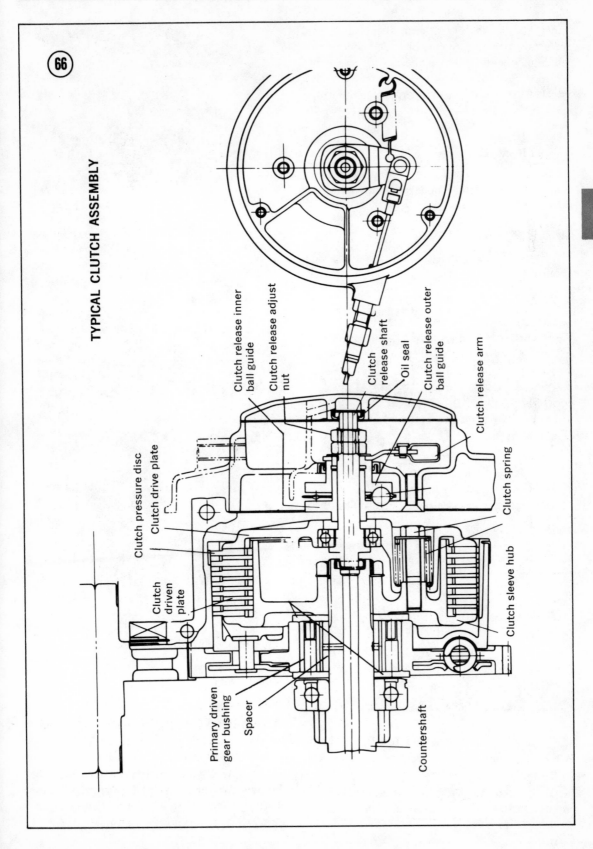

TYPICAL CLUTCH ASSEMBLY

66

3

Clutch release inner ball guide

Clutch release adjust nut

Clutch release shaft

Oil seal

Clutch release outer ball guide

Clutch release arm

Clutch pressure disc

Clutch drive plate

Clutch spring

Clutch driven plate

Clutch sleeve hub

Primary driven gear bushing

Spacer

Countershaft

rider pulls in the hand lever, the push crown presses against the pressure plate and compresses the clutch springs. When the springs are compressed, pressure is removed from the cork and steel plates, which then separate and interrupt power transmission.

Clutch Removal

Clutch removal and disassembly procedures vary between different models. Be sure to follow the correct procedure.

Models GT380 and GT550

1. Remove the right crankcase cover. See **Figure 67**.

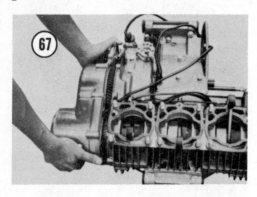

2. Remove the pressure plate (**Figure 68**), then each clutch plate.

3. Flatten the lockwasher (**Figure 69**), then hold the clutch hub and remove its retaining nut (**Figure 70**).

4. Pull off the clutch housing. On model GT550, remove the starter clutch together with the clutch housing (**Figure 71**).

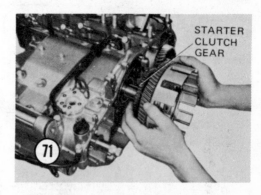

STARTER CLUTCH GEAR

5. **Figure 72** is an exploded view of a typical clutch on models GT380 and GT550.

Model GT750

1. Refer to **Figure 73**. Remove the clutch inspection cap, then loosen both shaft nuts (1) and remove the clutch lever (2).

2. Remove the clutch cover (3).

3. Refer to **Figure 74**. Remove six nuts, then remove the pressure plate (1) and release shaft (2).

4. Remove the steel and cork clutch plates.

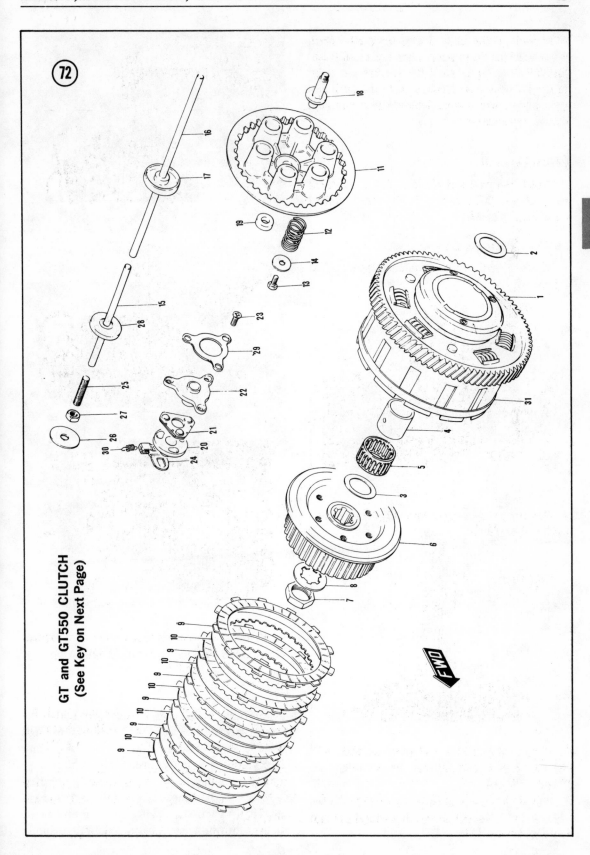

GT and GT550 CLUTCH
(See Key on Next Page)

GT380 and GT550 CLUTCH (See Diagram on Previous Page)

1. Primary driven gear assembly
2. Thrust washer
3. Thrust washer
4. Primary driven gear spacer
5. Driven gear needle bearing
6. Clutch sleeve hub
7. Clutch sleeve hub nut
8. Clutch sleeve hub washer
9. Cork plate
10. Clutch driven plate
11. Clutch pressure disc
12. Clutch spring
13. Bolt
14. Clutch spring washer
15. Clutch push rod (1)
16. Clutch push rod (2)
17. Clutch push rod oil seal
18. Clutch push piece
19. Clutch push piece oil seal
20. Clutch release outer ball guide
21. Clutch release ball
22. Clutch release inner ball guide
23. Screw
24. Clutch release arm
25. Clutch release adjusting screw
26. Clutch release screw washer
27. Nut
28. Ball guide dust seal
29. Ball guide gasket
30. Clutch release return spring
31. Clutch release V-ring

1. Shaft nut   2. Clutch lever   3. Cover

1. Pressure plate
2. Release shaft

5. Hold the clutch hub in position, then remove its retaining nut.

6. Refer to **Figure 75**. Remove the primary gear spacer (1) and bushing (2) by pulling with two bolts (3).

7. Remove the transmission oil reservoir plate.

8. **Figure 76** (page 27) is an exploded view of the clutch on model GT750.

Clutch Inspection

Measure the thickness of each drive plate in several places with calipers, as shown in **Figure 77**. Replace any plate which is worn unevenly, or worn or warped beyond the wear limit. See **Table 5**.

Measure the thickness and warpage (**Figure 78**) of each steel plate. Replace any plate that is worn or warped beyond the repair limit.

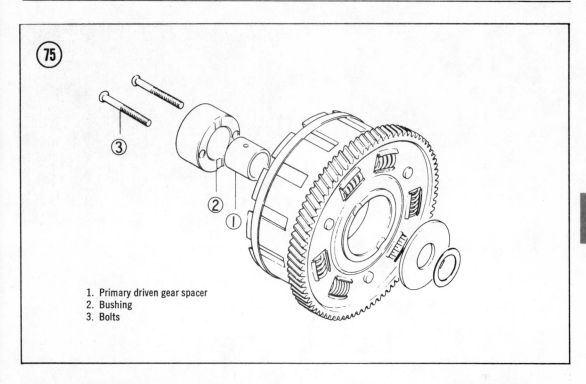

1. Primary driven gear spacer
2. Bushing
3. Bolts

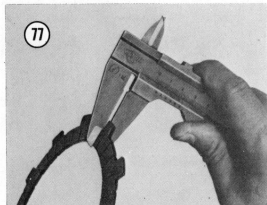

Table 5 DRIVE PLATE THICKNESS

Model	Standard Inch (Millimeters)	Wear Limit Inch (Millimeters)	Warpage Inch (Millimeters)
GT380	0.138 (3.5)	0.126 (3.2)	0.016 (0.4)
GT550	0.138 (3.5)	0.126 (3.2)	0.016 (0.4)
GT750	0.11-0.12 (2.9-3.1)	0.102 (2.7)	0.012 (0.3)

Measure free length of each clutch spring, as shown in **Figure 79**. If any spring is shorter than the service limit (**Table 6**), replace all springs.

Table 6 CLUTCH SPRING LENGTH

Model	Standard Inches (Millimeters)		Service Limit Inches (Millimeters)	
GT380	1.51	(38.4)	1.45	(36.9)
GT550	1.51	(38.4)	1.45	(36.9)
GT750	1.59	(40.4)	1.54	(39.0)

Inspect the primary gear teeth on the clutch housing. Minor burrs may be smoothed with an oilstone. Check for backlash between the

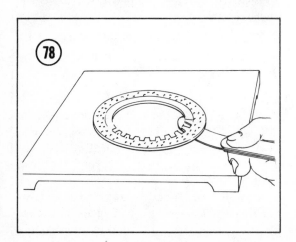

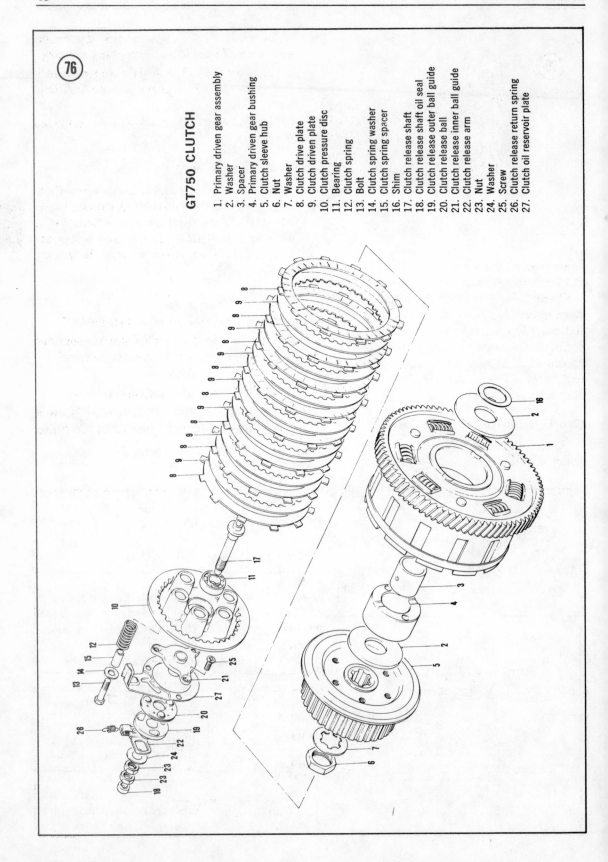

GT750 CLUTCH

1. Primary driven gear assembly
2. Washer
3. Spacer
4. Primary driven gear bushing
5. Clutch sleeve hub
6. Nut
7. Washer
8. Clutch drive plate
9. Clutch driven plate
10. Clutch pressure disc
11. Bearing
12. Clutch spring
13. Bolt
14. Clutch spring washer
15. Clutch spring spacer
16. Shim
17. Clutch release shaft
18. Clutch release shaft oil seal
19. Clutch release outer ball guide
20. Clutch release ball
21. Clutch release inner ball guide
22. Clutch release arm
23. Nut
24. Washer
25. Screw
26. Clutch release return spring
27. Clutch oil reservoir plate

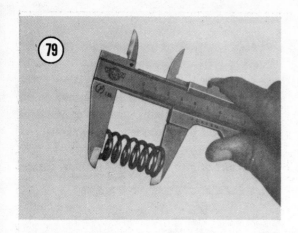

primary gears. Backlash greater than 0.006 inch (0.15 millimeter) should be considered excessive.

Check for worn splines in the clutch hub. If these splines are worn, clutch plates may stick and result in abrupt or rough clutch action.

Check the release mechanism for wear or looseness. If damage or excessive wear exists, replace the entire release assembly. Be sure that the pushrods are not bent.

Clutch Installation

Reverse the removal procedure to install the clutch. Observe the following notes:

1. On model GT550, be sure that the washer and spacer (**Figure 80**) are assembled correctly.

2. On model GT550, assemble the starter clutch and primary gear together before installing them.

3. The ends of the clutch release rods go toward the clutch.

Clutch Adjustment

Normal use of the clutch causes wear of the clutch plates and clutch cable. Therefore clutch adjustment is required from time to time. Clutch adjustment procedures differ slightly among the various models, so be sure to read the instructions carefully.

Model GT380

1. Refer to **Figure 81**. Loosen lock nut "A".

2. Turn in screw "B" until it bottoms against the pushrods, then back it off one-quarter turn.

3. Tighten lock nut "A".

4. Loosen clutch cable lock nut "a".

5. Turn cable adjuster "b" until there is about 0.16 inch (4 millimeters) play at the handlebar lever (**Figure 82**).

6. Tighten lock nut "a".

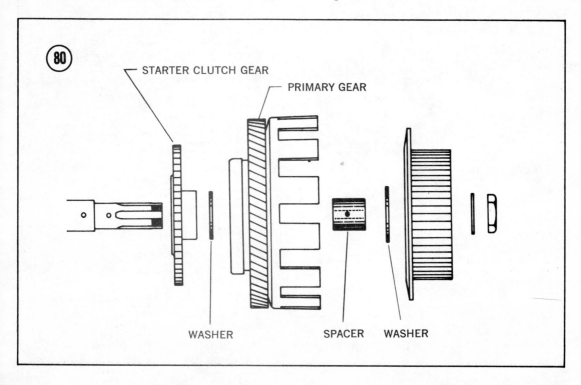

STARTER CLUTCH GEAR

PRIMARY GEAR

WASHER   SPACER   WASHER

A. Lock nut   B. Screw
a. Lock nut   b. Cable adjuster

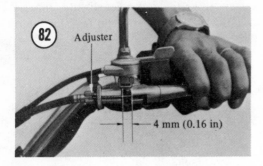

Adjuster

4 mm (0.16 in)

Model GT550

1. Refer to **Figure 83**. Be sure that the end of the clutch release lever aligns with the line on the crankcase. If not, correct its position by removing the release lever and adjusting the lever position as required.

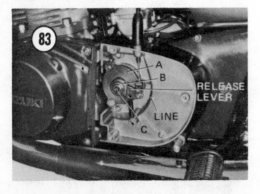

RELEASE LEVER
LINE

2. Loosen lock nut "B".

3. Turn in screw "C" until it seats lightly, then back it off one-half turn.

4. Tighten lock nut "B".

5. Turn the cable adjuster at the handlebar lever (Figure 82) to provide 0.016 inch (4 millimeters) free-play at the lever.

Model GT750

1. Refer to **Figure 84**. Loosen cable adjuster "A" until clutch cable "1" is slack.

A. Cable adjuster   2. Double nuts
1. Clutch cable   3. Release shaft

2. Loosen and adjust double nuts "2" until there is 0.008 inch (0.2 millimeter) end play in release shaft "3". Tighten both nuts and recheck end play.

3. Retighten cable adjuster "A".

4. Refer to **Figure 85**. Adjust cable adjuster "B" to provide 0.12 inch (3 millimeters) free-play at the handlebar lever.

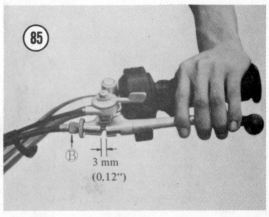

3 mm (0.12")

B. Cable adjuster

PRIMARY PINION

Removal

1. Using a hammer and a blunted chisel, flatten the tab on the primary pinion lockwasher.

2. Hold the connecting rod in position with a piston holder, then loosen the pinion nut.

3. Pull the pinion from the shaft by hand.

4. Remove the woodruff key.

Inspection

Check the gear teeth for wear or damage. Slight roughness may be smoothed with an oilstone. Replace the unit if damage cannot be smoothed.

Installation

Reverse the removal procedure to install the primary pinion. Be sure to check backlash after installation, as described in the foregoing section.

CRANKCASE

Crankcases on all models split into upper and lower halves. Crankcase disassembly is required for service on the crankshaft, bearings, transmission, and internal parts of the shifter and kickstarter.

Disassembly

1. There are numbers cast into the crankcase halves by each crankcase bolt. Remove the lower bolts (**Figure 86**) first, beginning with the highest number, then continue in descending order.

2. Remove the upper crankcase bolts (**Figure 87**). Begin with the highest number, then continue in descending order.

3. Place the engine on a workbench with the connecting rods upward.

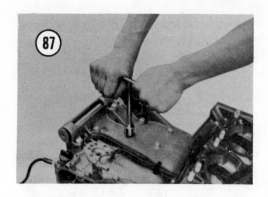

4. Pull the upper crankcase half away, as shown in **Figure 88**. It may be necessary to tap the projecting lugs lightly with a rubber mallet to break the halves apart.

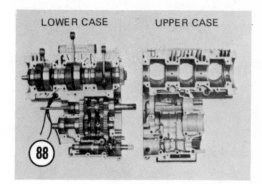

LOWER CASE   UPPER CASE

Inspection

Inspect the crankcase halves for damage, particularly around the sealing surfaces. Be sure that all lubricant passages are clean and unobstructed. Clean any gasket cement from the mating surfaces.

Reassembly

Reverse the disassembly procedure to assemble the crankcase halves. Pay particular attention to the following points.

1. Apply a suitable gasket cement to the upper crankcase half joining surfaces, and allow the cement to become tacky before assembly.

2. Tap the uppermost crankcase half with a soft mallet, if necessary, to fit the two halves together. Be sure that the dowel pins are aligned.

3. Rotate the crankshaft and transmission shaft by hand to check for smooth movement. Do not proceed if the shafts don't turn smoothly.

4. Tighten crankcase bolts first by running them down snug, then tightening the upper ones in the order marked. Repeat the procedure on the lower bolts. Torque bolts. See **Table 7**.

Table 7   CRANKCASE BOLT TORQUES

| | Torque | |
Size	Pound-feet	(Kilogram-centimeters)
6 millimeter	4.4-7.2	(60-100)
8 millimeter	9.4-16.6	(130-230)
10 millimeter	18.1-28.9	(250-400)

NOTE: *If model GT750 crankcase halves are replaced, refer to special instructions in the transmission section of this book.*

CRANKSHAFT

The crankshaft operates under conditions of high stress. Dimensional tolerances are critical. It is necessary to locate and correct crankshaft defects to prevent more serious trouble later.

Crankshaft Inspection

Measure crankshaft alignment as shown in **Figure 89**. Mount the crankshaft in a lathe, V-blocks, or other suitable centering device. Rotate the crankshaft through a complete revolution and measure runout as shown by the dial indicators. Measure runout at each end of the crankshaft. Repair or replace the crankshaft if runout exceeds the repair limit (**Table 8**).

Table 8   CRANKSHAFT RUNOUT

| | Repair Limit | |
Model	Inch	(Millimeter)
GT380	0.002	(0.05)
GT550	0.002	(0.05)
GT750	0.003	(0.08)

To correct runout, tap the crank wheels with a brass or lead mallet, as required. Check the crankshaft assembly after each adjustment.

The simplest method for determining if there is excessive wear in the connecting rod big end bearings is to measure the total distance that the connecting rod may be shaken from side to side

(**Figure 90**). To measure this distance, mount the crankshaft assembly in a suitable jig. Measure the total travel (connecting rod shake) of the upper end of the connecting rod as you move it from side to side. Hold the big end of the rod to one side so that you don't mistake big end side play for wear. Repair or replace the crankshaft assembly if connecting rod shake exceeds 0.12 inch (3.0 millimeters).

Be sure that the connecting rods are not bent or twisted. To check for bent connecting rods, assemble the crankcase, crankshaft, pistons, and cylinders. Do not install piston rings. While turning the engine, check to be sure that each piston is not pressed against either side of its cylinder.

Be sure that all crankshaft oil seals are in good condition. Primary compression leakage will occur in the event of defective oil seals.

It is usually better to replace the crankshaft rather than to attempt repairs which require its disassembly. Special tools and alignment fixtures are required.

Crankshaft Installation

1. Thoroughly clean and lubricate all parts before installation.

2. Be sure that all oil seals are pushed as close to the bearings as possible (**Figure 91**).

3. Pins on crankshaft bearings should be placed in the corresponding grooves in the lower crankcase half (**Figure 92**).

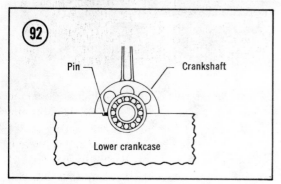

4. Punch marks (1) on bearings in model GT750 must align with the crankcase mating surface (**Figure 93**).

TRANSMISSION

Operating and service procedures are similar for all transmissions; differences are pointed out where the exist. During transmission disassembly, take careful note of the location and

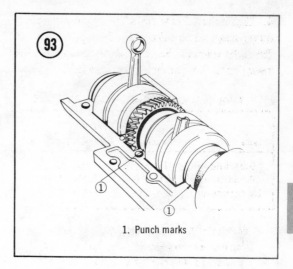

1. Punch marks

orientation of each part. **Figures 94A through 94F** illustrate power flow in the various gears of a typical transmission. **Figures 95** (p. 56), **96** (pp. 57-58), and **97** (p. 59) are exploded views of transmissions in models GT380, GT550, and GT750, respectively. Refer to these illustrations during disassembly and reassembly.

Disassembly

Remove each gear and bearing from the shafts by removing the snap rings which retain them. Some gears, such as 2nd driven gear, may have to be pressed from the shaft. Take particular care to observe the location and orientation of all small parts such as thrust washers.

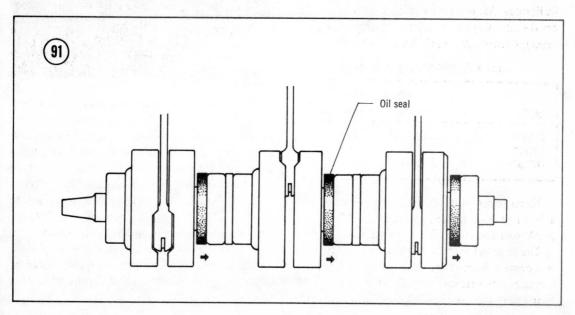

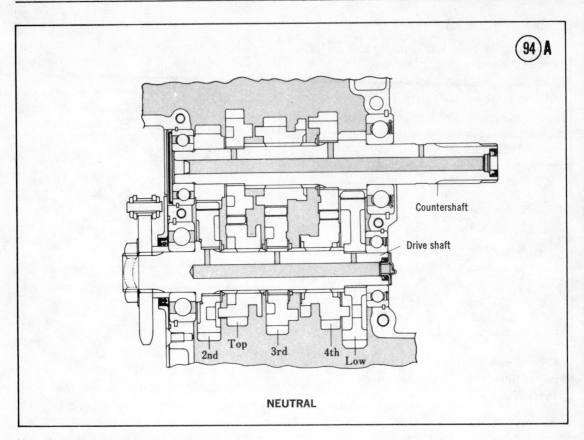

Countershaft

Drive shaft

2nd Top 3rd 4th Low

NEUTRAL

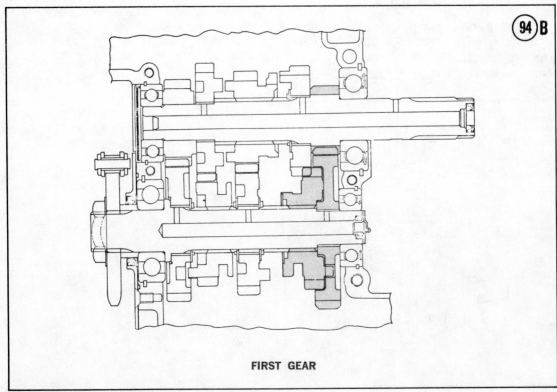

FIRST GEAR

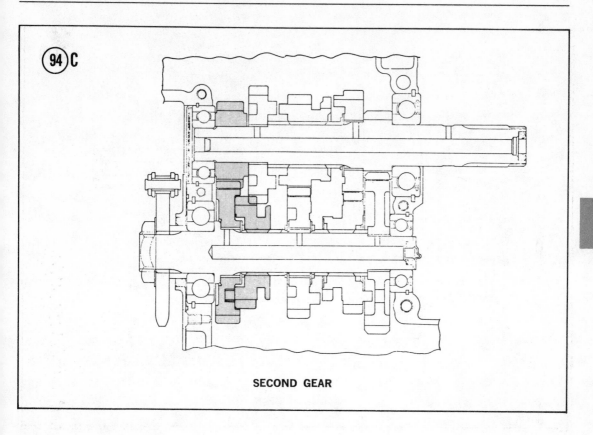

SECOND GEAR

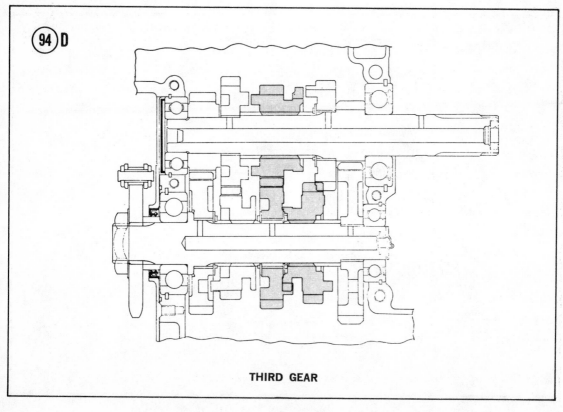

THIRD GEAR

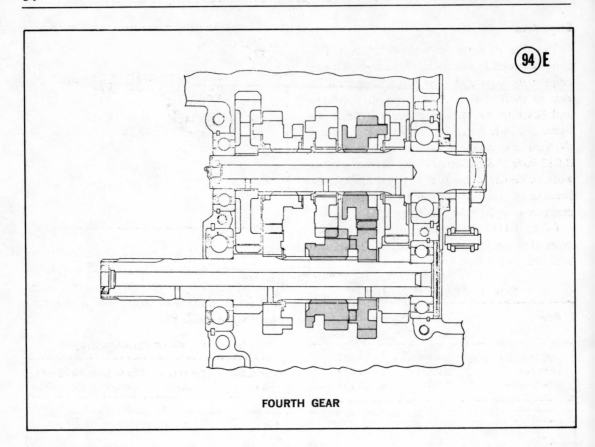

FOURTH GEAR

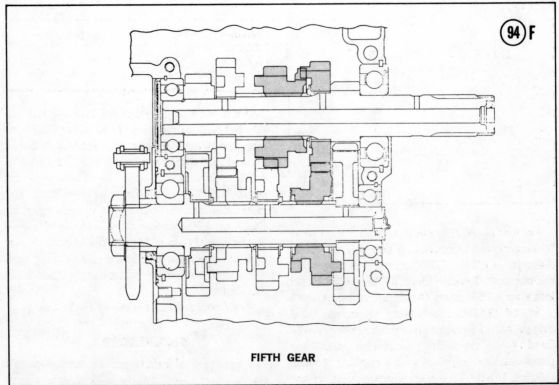

FIFTH GEAR

Inspection

Examine all parts for wear or damage. Pay close attention to the teeth on the dog clutches, chipped or damaged gear teeth, and wear in gear or shaft splines. Also check the bushings and bearings for wear. Measure clearance between the shift forks and the grooves. Replace the gear and/or the fork if clearance exceeds 0.032 inch (0.8 millimeter). Replace any other worn or damaged parts. If any gear is replaced because of worn or damaged teeth, it is good practice to replace the mating gear also.

On model GT750, measure backlash between gears as shown in **Figure 98**. Replace gears with backlash greater than specified in **Table 9**.

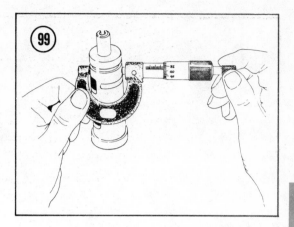

replaced, note that 2 gears are supplied as replacements. Each gear has a painted mark on it. There is also a painted spot on the side of the right lower crankcase. Select the proper gear according to **Table 10**.

Table 9   GEAR BACKLASH

Gear	Backlash Limit	
	Inch	(Millimeter)
1st, 2nd, 3rd	0.002	(0.05)
Kick gear	0.002	(0.05)
All others	0.004	(0.10)

Table 10   GEAR IDENTIFICATION

Crankcase Color	1st Driven Gear	2nd Driven Gear	Kickstarter Drive Gear
Brown Black Red Yellow	Yellow	Yellow	Brown
Yellow Blue Green White	White	White	Yellow

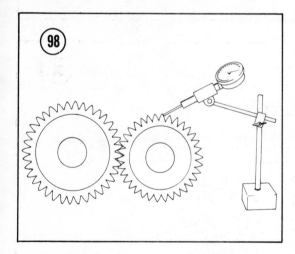

On model GT750, measure shifter cam wear by measuring its diameter (**Figure 99**). Standard diameter is 1.768 - 1.771 inches (44.90 - 44.98 millimeters). Replace the cam if it is worn to less than 1.760 inches (44.70 millimeters).

Model GT750 crankcases, 1st driven, 2nd driven, and kickstarter drive gears are selectively fitted. If the crankcase is replaced, install the gears which are supplied with it in place of those existing. If any of the gears mentioned above are

If it is necessary to press 2nd driven gear back into position on models GT550 or GT750, note that dimensions are critical. Distance between 1st and 2nd gears on the shaft must be 4.488 to 4.492 inches (114.0 to 114.1 millimeters) for model GT550, as shown in **Figure 100**. On model GT750, distance between gears must be 4.307 to 4.311 inches (109.4 to 109.5 millimeters), as shown in **Figure 101**. Apply thread lock cement to the bore in the gear before pressing it onto the shaft. Do not apply cement to the shaft.

Apply thread lock cement to all threads.

KICKSTARTER

Three types of kickstarters are used, depending on engine size. All types have parts which

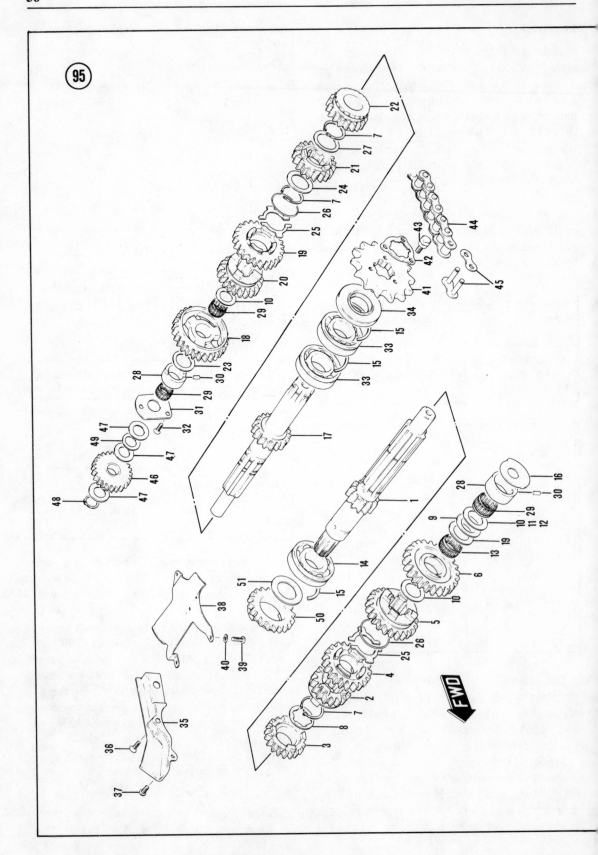

96

3

GT380 TRANSMISSION

1. Countershaft
2. 2nd drive gear
3. 3rd drive gear
4. 4th drive gear
5. 5th drive gear
6. 6th drive gear
7. 3rd drive gear circlip
8. 3rd drive gear lockwasher
9. 6th drive gear thrust washer
10. 6th drive gear thrust washer
11. 6th drive gear thrust washer
12. 6th drive gear thrust washer
13. 6th drive gear bearing
14. Countershaft bearing
15. Countershaft C-ring
16. Countershaft retainer
17. Driveshaft
18. 1st driven gear
19. 2nd driven gear
20. 3rd driven gear
21. 4th driven gear
22. 5th driven gear
23. 1st driven gear thrust washer
24. 4th driven gear RH washer
25. 2nd driven gear ring
26. 2nd driven gear circlip
27. 4th driven gear thrust washer
28. Transmission shaft bushing
29. Transmission shaft bearing
30. Transmission shaft bushing pin
31. Driveshaft retainer
32. Retainer screw
33. Bearing
34. Driveshaft oil seal
35. Oil reservoir cup
36. Screw
37. Screw
38. Oil guide plate
39. Oil guide plate screw
40. Lockwasher
41. Engine sprocket
42. Engine sprocket plate
43. Plate bolt
44. Drive chain assembly
45. Chain joint
46. Kickstarter idle gear
47. Kick idle gear thrust washer
48. Idle gear circlip
49. Idle gear wave washer
50. Kickstarter driven gear
51. Kickstarter driven washer

GT550 TRANSMISSION (See Diagram on Next Page)

1. Countershaft assembly
2. Countershaft
3. 2nd drive gear
4. 3rd drive gear
5. 4th drive gear
6. 5th drive gear
7. 4th drive gear washer
8. 4th drive gear circlip
9. Driveshaft
10. 1st driven gear
11. 2nd driven gear
12. 3rd driven gear
13. 4th driven gear
14. 5th driven gear
15. 1st driven gear washer
16. 2nd driven gear LH washer
17. 3rd driven gear washer
18. Driven gear circlip
19. Countershaft RH bearing
20. Countershaft LH bearing
21. Driveshaft RH bearing
22. Driveshaft bearing RH bushing
23. Driveshaft RH bearing (1)
24. Driveshaft LH bearing (2)
25. Countershaft bearing RH C-ring
26. Countershaft bearing LH C-ring
27. Driveshaft bearing LH C-ring
28. Driveshaft bushing C-ring
29. Driveshaft oil seal
30. Driveshaft bushing dowel pin
31. Countershaft oil reserver plug
32. Oil guide plate oil seal
33. Oil reservoir plate
34. Screw
35. Screw
36. Oil guide plate
37. Oil guide plate screw
38. Lockwasher
39. Engine sprocket
40. Engine sprocket plate
41. Sprocket plate bolt
42. Engine sprocket washer
43. Drive chain assembly
44. Chain joint

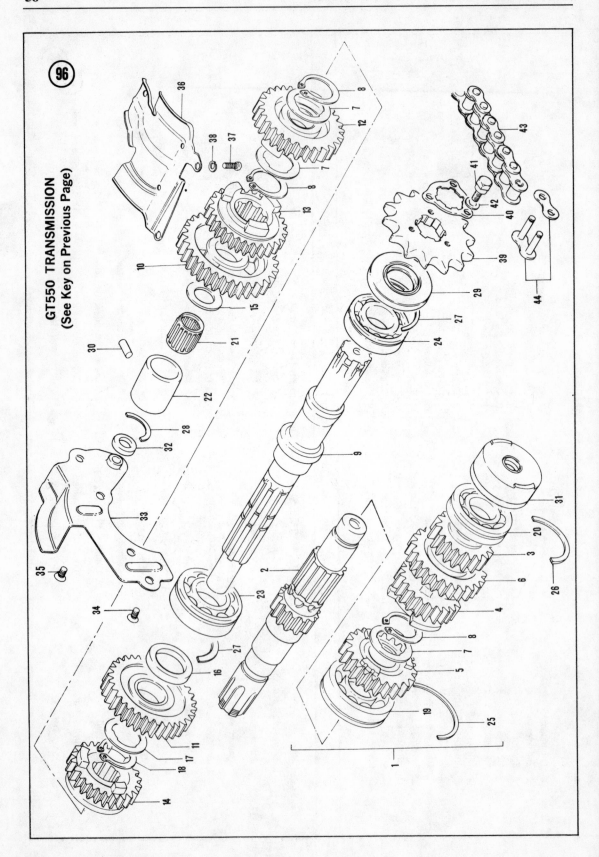

96

GT550 TRANSMISSION
(See Key on Previous Page)

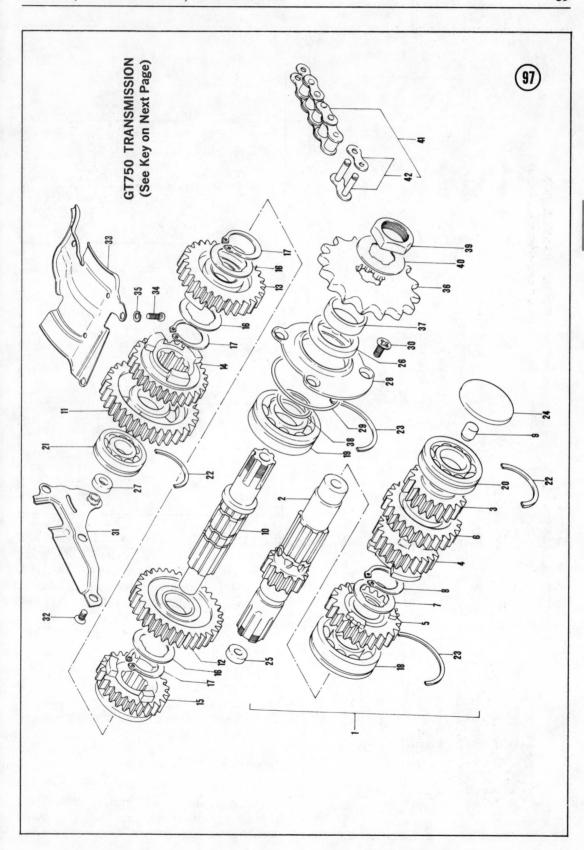

GT750 TRANSMISSION
(See Key on Next Page)

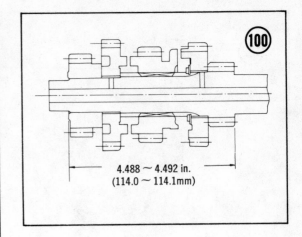

(97)

GT750 TRANSMISSION (See Diagram on Previous Page)

1. Countershaft assembly
2. Countershaft
3. 2nd drive gear
4. 3rd drive gear
5. 4th drive gear
6. 5th drive gear
7. 4th drive gear washer
8. 4th drive gear circlip
9. Countershaft plug
10. Driveshaft
11. 1st driven gear
12. 2nd driven gear
13. 3rd driven gear
14. 4th driven gear
15. 5th driven gear
16. Driven gear washer
17. Driven gear circlip
18. Countershaft RH bearing
19. Countershaft LH bearing
20. Countershaft LH bearing
21. Driveshaft RH bearing
22. C-ring
23. C-ring
24. Countershaft bearing plug
25. Countershaft oil seal
26. Driveshaft oil seal
27. Oil guide plate oil seal
28. Driveshaft oil seal retainer
29. O-ring
30. Screw
31. Oil reservoir plate
32. Screw
33. Oil guide plate
34. Oil guide plate screw
35. Lockwasher
36. Engine sprocket
37. Engine sprocket spacer
38. O-ring
39. Nut
40. Washer
41. Drive chain
42. Chain joint

(100)

4.488 ~ 4.492 in.
(114.0 ~ 114.1mm)

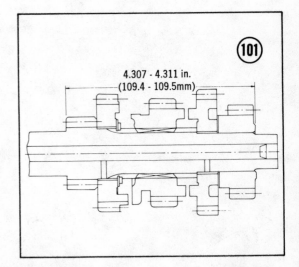

(101)

4.307 - 4.311 in.
(109.4 - 109.5mm)

can be serviced without major disassembly of the engine, and also parts which require splitting of the crankcase for service. **Figures 102, 103, and 104** are exploded views of kickstarters on models GT380, GT550, and GT750, respectively.

Disassembly

Refer to the applicable instructions for splitting the crankcase. All kickstarter parts can be removed easily. Note carefully the locations of the various small parts, such as thrust washers, as you remove them.

Inspection

Check gear teeth for wear or damage. Kickstarter gears should slide freely on their shafts. Any spring showing evidence of fatigue or cracks should be replaced.

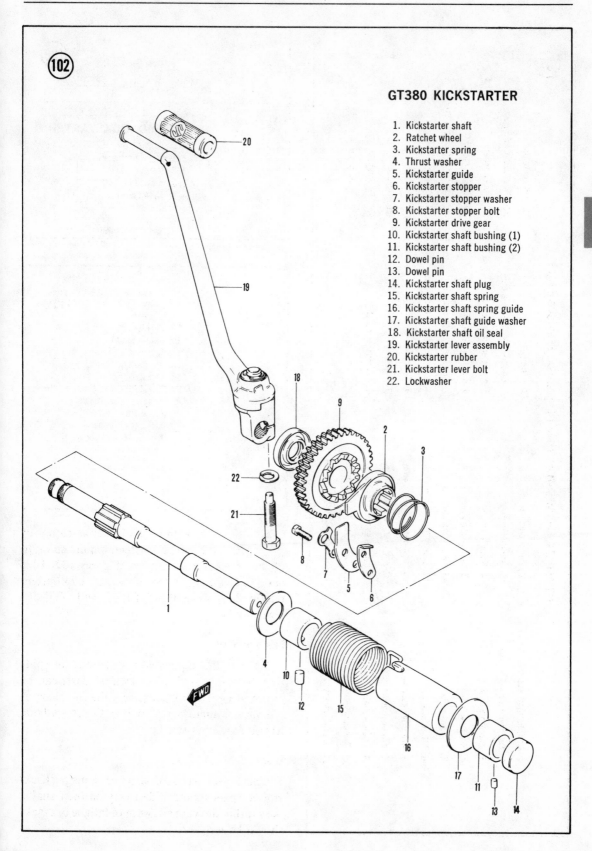

⑩

GT380 KICKSTARTER

1. Kickstarter shaft
2. Ratchet wheel
3. Kickstarter spring
4. Thrust washer
5. Kickstarter guide
6. Kickstarter stopper
7. Kickstarter stopper washer
8. Kickstarter stopper bolt
9. Kickstarter drive gear
10. Kickstarter shaft bushing (1)
11. Kickstarter shaft bushing (2)
12. Dowel pin
13. Dowel pin
14. Kickstarter shaft plug
15. Kickstarter shaft spring
16. Kickstarter shaft spring guide
17. Kickstarter shaft guide washer
18. Kickstarter shaft oil seal
19. Kickstarter lever assembly
20. Kickstarter rubber
21. Kickstarter lever bolt
22. Lockwasher

3

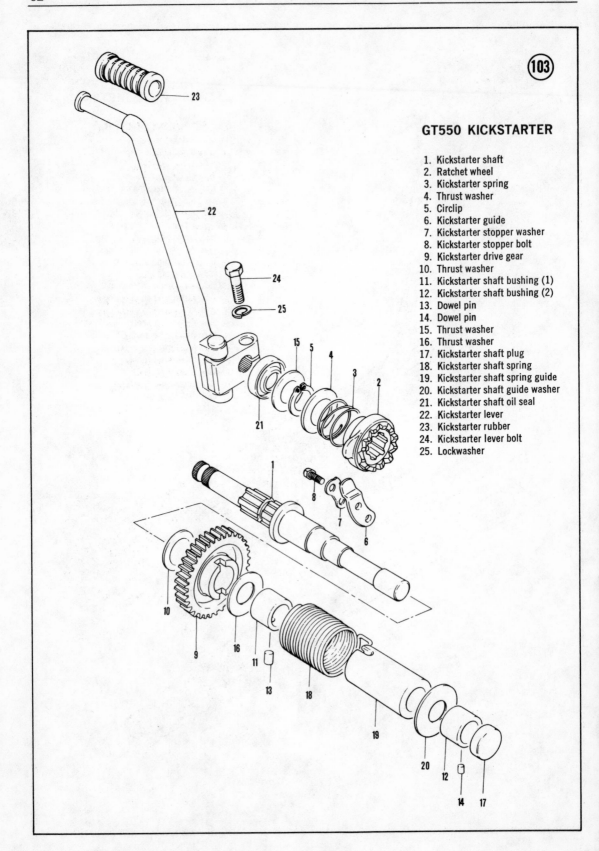

(103)

GT550 KICKSTARTER

 1. Kickstarter shaft
 2. Ratchet wheel
 3. Kickstarter spring
 4. Thrust washer
 5. Circlip
 6. Kickstarter guide
 7. Kickstarter stopper washer
 8. Kickstarter stopper bolt
 9. Kickstarter drive gear
10. Thrust washer
11. Kickstarter shaft bushing (1)
12. Kickstarter shaft bushing (2)
13. Dowel pin
14. Dowel pin
15. Thrust washer
16. Thrust washer
17. Kickstarter shaft plug
18. Kickstarter shaft spring
19. Kickstarter shaft spring guide
20. Kickstarter shaft guide washer
21. Kickstarter shaft oil seal
22. Kickstarter lever
23. Kickstarter rubber
24. Kickstarter lever bolt
25. Lockwasher

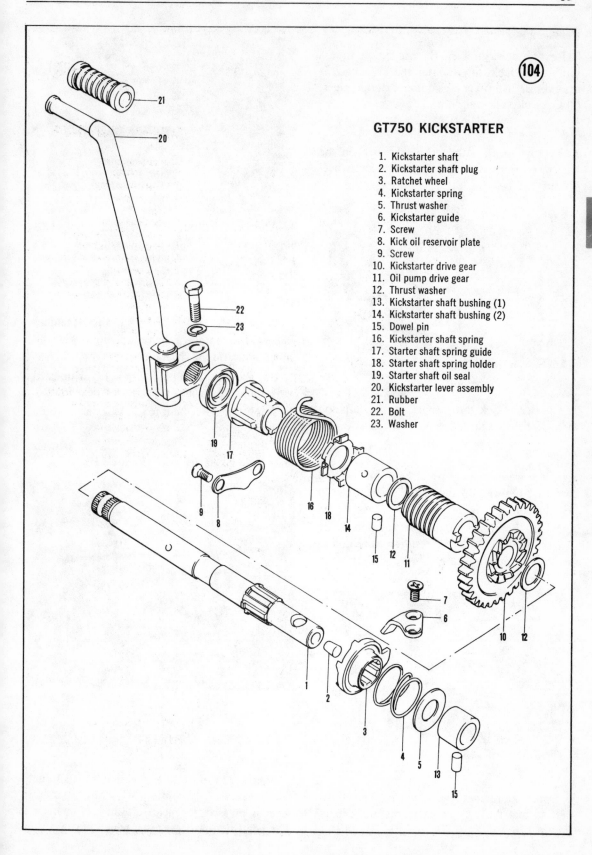

(104)

GT750 KICKSTARTER

1. Kickstarter shaft
2. Kickstarter shaft plug
3. Ratchet wheel
4. Kickstarter spring
5. Thrust washer
6. Kickstarter guide
7. Screw
8. Kick oil reservoir plate
9. Screw
10. Kickstarter drive gear
11. Oil pump drive gear
12. Thrust washer
13. Kickstarter shaft bushing (1)
14. Kickstarter shaft bushing (2)
15. Dowel pin
16. Kickstarter shaft spring
17. Starter shaft spring guide
18. Starter shaft spring holder
19. Starter shaft oil seal
20. Kickstarter lever assembly
21. Rubber
22. Bolt
23. Washer

3

Reassembly

Reverse the disassembly procedure to assemble the kickstarter. After the crankcase is assembled, install the kickstarter external parts. Observe the following notes:

Model GT380

1. Be sure to align the punched mark on the kickstarter shaft with that on the ratchet wheel (**Figure 105**).

2. Check the kickstarter shaft after installation to be sure that it turns freely.

Model GT550

1. There are 2 bushings which must be installed correctly. **Figure 106** shows the correct way to install them.

2. When the crankcase halves are joined, be sure that the end of the kickstarter spring is in the hole in the crankcase (**Figure 107**).

3. Install the ratchet wheel over the kickstarter shaft so that the two punch marks are aligned (**Figure 108**).

PUNCH MARKS

4. After installation, turn the kickstarter shaft approximately ¾ turn counterclockwise, then set the ratchet wheel so that its boss engages the stop.

Model GT750

1. Refer to **Figure 109** (page 66). Install ratchet wheel (1) so that the punch mark aligns with the punch mark on the shaft (2).

2. Be sure that the oil guide hole (3) is upward when the ratchet wheel (1) contacts the guide (4).

3. Apply thread cement to the kickstarter guide screws.

4. Align the punch marks on the kickstarter shaft and kickstarter lever (**Figure 110**).

SHIFTER

Operation

Figure 111 illustrates the major functional components of the shifter. When the gearshift lever is pressed, the gearshift shaft (1) rotates. The gearshift pawl gear (4), which engages the

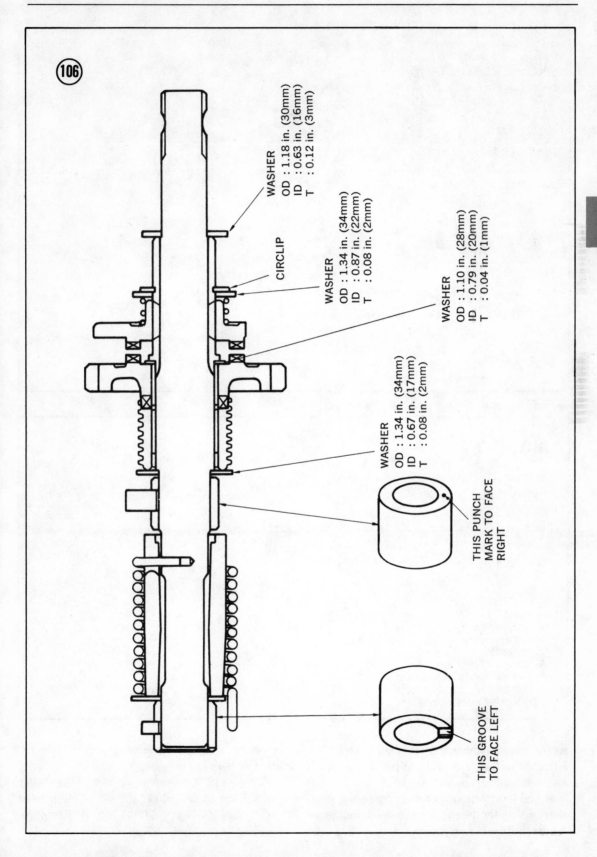

WASHER
OD : 1.18 in. (30mm)
ID : 0.63 in. (16mm)
T : 0.12 in. (3mm)

CIRCLIP

WASHER
OD : 1.34 in. (34mm)
ID : 0.87 in. (22mm)
T : 0.08 in. (2mm)

WASHER
OD : 1.10 in. (28mm)
ID : 0.79 in. (20mm)
T : 0.04 in. (1mm)

WASHER
OD : 1.34 in. (34mm)
ID : 0.67 in. (17mm)
T : 0.08 in. (2mm)

THIS PUNCH
MARK TO FACE
RIGHT

THIS GROOVE
TO FACE LEFT

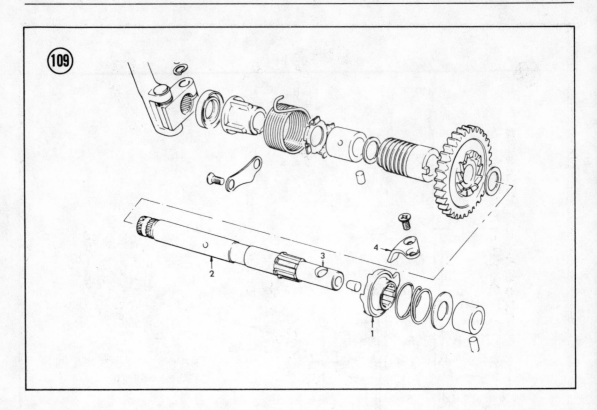

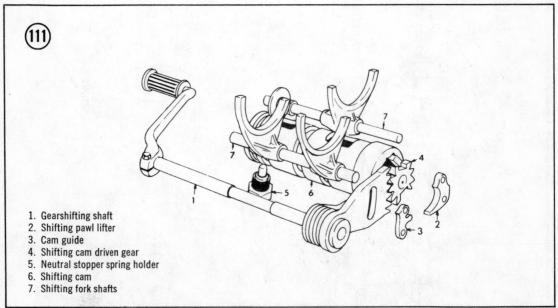

1. Gearshifting shaft
2. Shifting pawl lifter
3. Cam guide
4. Shifting cam driven gear
5. Neutral stopper spring holder
6. Shifting cam
7. Shifting fork shafts

sector gear on the gearshift shaft, turns also. Attached to the pawl gear are two pawls which rotate the shift cam (6). Grooves on the shift cam are so arranged that rotation of the gearshift cam causes the shift forks to move sideways. As the shift forks move sideways, they slide their associated gears into engagement or disengagement as required to select the desired gear ratio.

Figure 112 is an exploded view of the shifter mechanism on model GT380. The shifter used on models GT550 and GT750 is shown in **Figure 113** (pages 68-69).

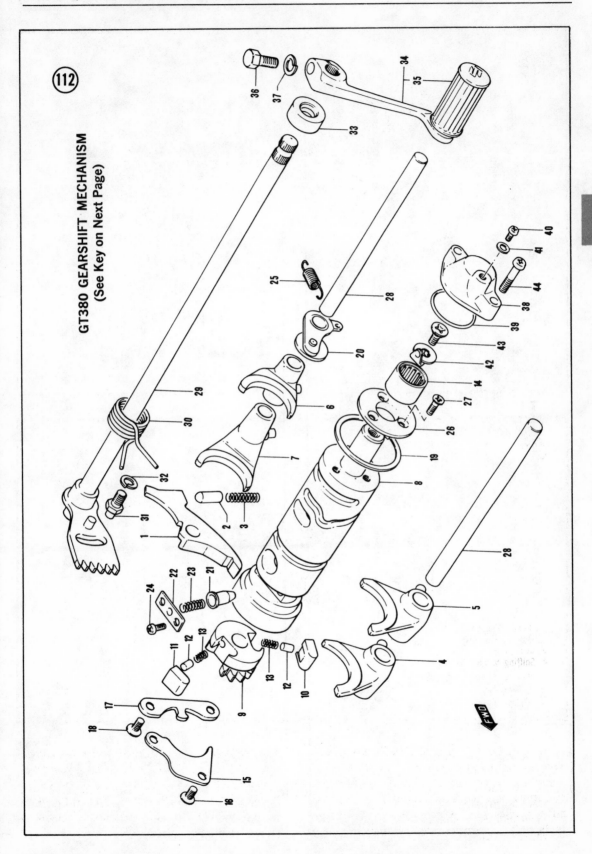

(112)

GT380 GEARSHIFT MECHANISM
(See Key on Next Page)

3

GT380 GEARSHIFT MECHANISM (See Diagram on Previous Page)

1. Transmission brake shoe
2. Transmission brake shoe tappet
3. Brake shoe tappet spring
4. 2nd drive gear shifting fork
5. 3rd drive gear shifting fork
6. 5th driven gear shifting fork
7. 5th drive gear shifting fork
8. Gear shifting cam
9. Gear shifting cam driven gear
10. Gear shifting pawl (1)
11. Gear shifting pawl (2)
12. Gear shifting pawl click pin
13. Pawl return spring
14. Gear shifting cam bearing
15. Gear shifting pawl lifter
16. Screw
17. Gear shifting cam guide
18. Screw
19. Gear shifting cam thrust washer
20. Gear shifting cam stopper
21. Gear shifting cam stopper
22. Stopper spring holder
23. Cam stopper spring
24. Spring holder screw
25. Stopper arm spring
26. Stopper plate plate
27. Stopper plate screw
28. Gear shifting fork shaft
29. Gear shifting shaft
30. Return spring
31. Shifting arm stopper
32. Lockwasher
33. Gear shifting shaft oil seal
34. Gear shifting lever assembly
35. Gear shifting pedal rubber
36. Bolt
37. Lockwasher
38. Gear shifting switch body
39. O-ring
40. Screw
41. Washer
42. Gear shifting switch contact
43. Screw
44. Screw

GT550 AND GT750 GEARSHIFT MECHANISM

1. Gear shifting fork (1)
2. Gear shifting fork (2)
3. Gear shifting fork shaft
4. Shifting cam
5. Shifting cam bearing
6. Shifting cam driven gear
7. Shifting pawl (1)
8. Shifting pawl (2)
9. Shifting pawl pin
10. Shifting pawl return spring
11. Shifting pawl guide
12. Screw
13. Shifting cam guide
14. Screw
15. Thrust washer
16. Shifting cam stopper
17. Stopper spring holder
18. Shifting cam stopper spring
19. Spring holder washer
20. Shifting cam stopper
21. Shifting cam stopper plate
22. Cam stopper arm spring
23. Screw
24. Gear shifting shaft
25. Shifting shaft return spring
26. Shifting arm stopper
27. Lockwasher
28. Gear shifting shaft oil seal
29. Gear shifting lever
30. Shifting lever rubber
31. Bolt
32. Lockwasher
33. Gear shifting switch body
34. O-ring
35. Screw
36. Washer
37. Gear shifting switch contact
38. Screw
39. Screw

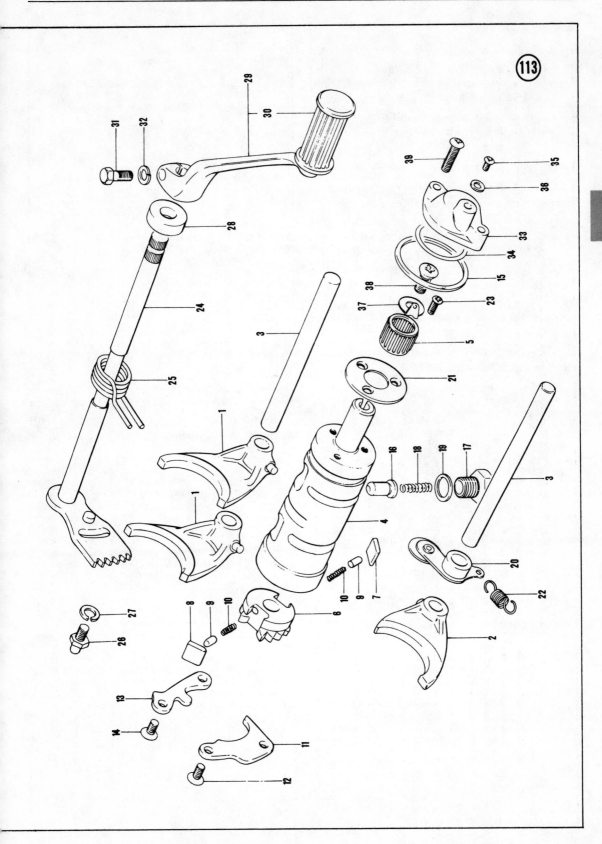

Inspection

Check the shift forks for burrs or scratches. Be sure that the shift fork shafts are not bent. Examine the shift pawl stopper for wear. Check that the shift pawl lifter is not worn. Check springs for evidence of fatigue or cracks. Replace any worn or damaged parts.

OIL SEALS

Oil seals perform several important functions. The first is to prevent loss of oil from the engine. Oil seals also prevent primary compression leakage from the crank chamber, which is essential to two-stroke engine operation. Finally, oil seals also prevent entry of foreign matter into the working parts of the engine. Always replace the oil seals upon engine reassembly.

Observe the following notes when you install the oil seals.

1. Always lubricate the oil seal lips with grease before installation (**Figure 114**).

2. Be very sure that the oil seal is not cocked in its bore. A light coating of grease on the outside surface of the seal will aid installation.

3. Be sure that the lips are not bent (**Figure 115**).

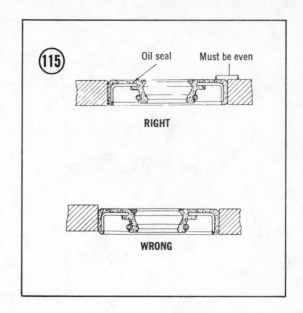

BEARINGS

Always check bearing condition upon engine reassembly. To do so, first clean the bearing thoroughly in solvent, dry it, then lubricate it. Spin the bearing (**Figure 116**), and check for abnormal noise or roughness as it coasts down. Do not spin a dry bearing.

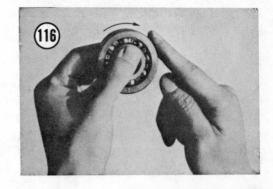

LIQUID COOLING SYSTEM

4

Model GT750 has a liquid cooling system similar to that of a conventional automobile. An engine-driven water pump circulates coolant through the cylinder head and cylinder jackets, then through an aluminum radiator. An auxiliary fan, controlled by a thermoswitch, provides additional airflow through the radiator during periods of high engine temperature.

RADIATOR

The radiator is of conventional corrugated fin and tube construction. Its approximate dimensions are 9.5 inches (240 millimeters) high, 17 inches (430 millimeters) wide, and 2.3 inches (60 millimeters) thick.

Removal

1. Drain coolant.
2. Remove the fuel tank.
3. Loosen necessary clamps, then remove the radiator inlet and outlet hoses, surge tank and its hose, and the inlet tube.
4. Remove the fan and fan shroud.
5. Remove the radiator guard.
6. Remove the radiator. Note the position of each mounting shim as it is removed.

Inspection

1. Check the radiator for leakage at all seams and in the core. Replace the radiator in the event of leaks.
2. Check the core for clogging by mud, insects, or any other foreign material which might impede proper airflow. A stream of water from a garden hose directed at the back side of the radiator will usually clean away any foreign matter.
3. Straighten any bent cooling fins.

Installation

Reverse the removal procedure to install the radiator. Note that the radiator is aluminum; therefore particular attention must be paid to its proper installation to avoid stress concentrations which could lead to cracks.

There are 3 different thicknesses of mounting shims. See **Table 1**.

Table 1   SHIM THICKNESS

Shim	Thickness	
	Inch	(Millimeter)
A	0.079	(2.0)
B	0.063	(1.6)
C	0.031	(0.8)

Refer to **Figure 1** for shim location. The upper and/or lower tanks may or may not be marked with a white circle. Refer to **Table 2** for washer locations.

Table 2   WASHER LOCATIONS

Tank and Mark	Shim Location	
	Inside	Outside
Upper with circle	A	B
Upper without circle	B	B
Lower with circle	B	A
Lower without circle	B	B

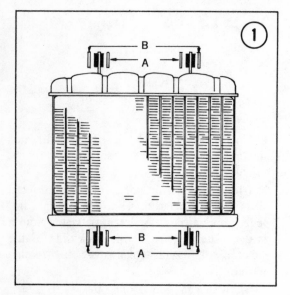

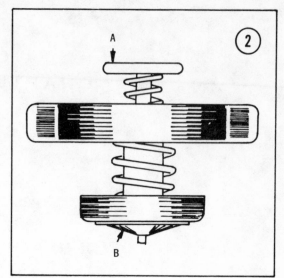

pressure relief valve should open at 12.8 ± 1.4 pounds per square inch (0.9 ± 0.1 kilogram per square centimeter). If no pressure tester is available, support the valve in an inverted position and place weights upon the valve as shown in **Figure 3**. The valve should open at approximately 15.4 pounds (7 kilograms).

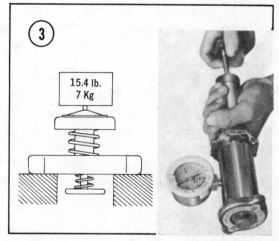

Use shim "C" as required to fill any of the remaining gap.

RADIATOR CAP

The radiator cap (**Figure 2**) is equipped with three valves. The first is a pressure release valve which opens if cooling system pressure exceeds approximately 13 pounds per square inch (0.9 kilogram per square centimeter). Valve "A" operates by finger pressure to bleed any residual pressure from the system before cap removal. Valve "B" acts as a vacuum breaker. As system pressure drops as a result of cooling and contraction, valve "B" opens to prevent possible damage to the radiator.

Check the pressure cap for opening pressure, using a conventional radiator cap tester. The

THERMOSTAT

A thermostat (**Figure 4**) controls coolant flow through the radiator, thereby maintaining a more constant engine temperature. At coolant temperatures of 180 degrees F (82 degrees C) or lower, the thermostat closes, blocking coolant flow to the radiator. Coolant then flows through

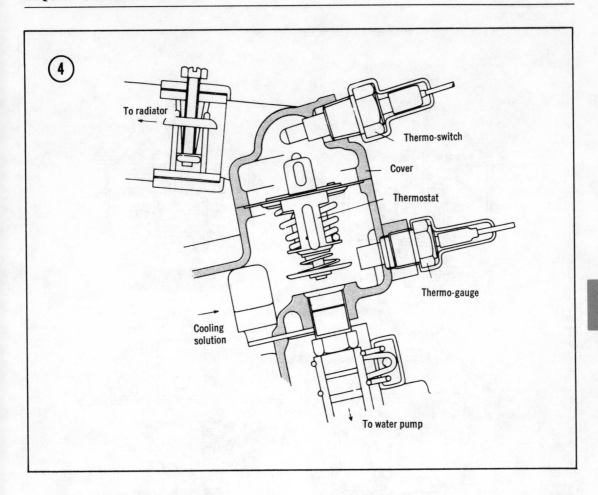

④ To radiator

Thermo-switch

Cover

Thermostat

Thermo-gauge

Cooling solution

To water pump

4

a bypass duct back to the engine. As coolant temperature rises to 180 degrees F (82 degrees C), the thermostat valve begins to open, and allows some coolant to flow through the radiator. When coolant temperature reaches 203 degrees F (95 degrees C), the thermostat opens completely, closing the bypass and directing all coolant through the radiator. Expansion and contraction of a wax pellet provides operating power for the thermostat (**Figure 5**).

Service on the thermostat is limited to checking the pellet for cracks, and measuring its operating temperature. Immerse the thermostat in a vessel of water (**Figure 6**) together with an accurate thermometer. Heat the water, and stir continuously to maintain a uniform temperature. If the valve is operating properly, it will begin to open at 180 degrees F (82 degrees C), and be fully open at 203 degrees F (95 degrees C). Valve stroke at full opening is 0.3 inch (8 millimeters).

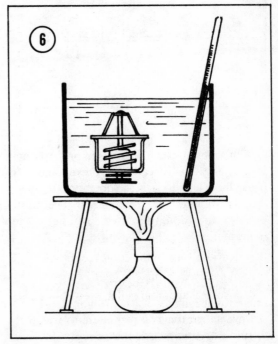

⑥

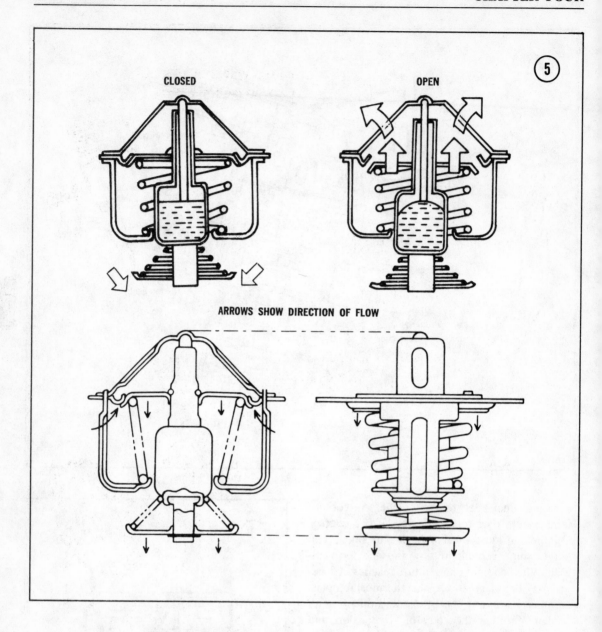

CLOSED   OPEN

ARROWS SHOW DIRECTION OF FLOW

A thermostat which operates improperly may lead to engine overheating or overcooling. Replace the thermostat if its operating temperatures vary appreciably from normal. Thermostat troubles are usually caused by one of the following:

a. Rust or scale in the coolant solution

b. Weakened spring

c. Wax leakage from pellet

Reverse the removal procedure to install the thermostat. Always use a new gasket.

WATER PUMP

The water pump (**Figure 7**) is mounted in the transmission chamber at the bottom of the engine. It is of centrifugal type, with a six-blade impeller.

Removal

1. Drain the coolant.

2. Remove both central mufflers.

3. Remove the water pump cover. Be careful not to damage its gasket surface.

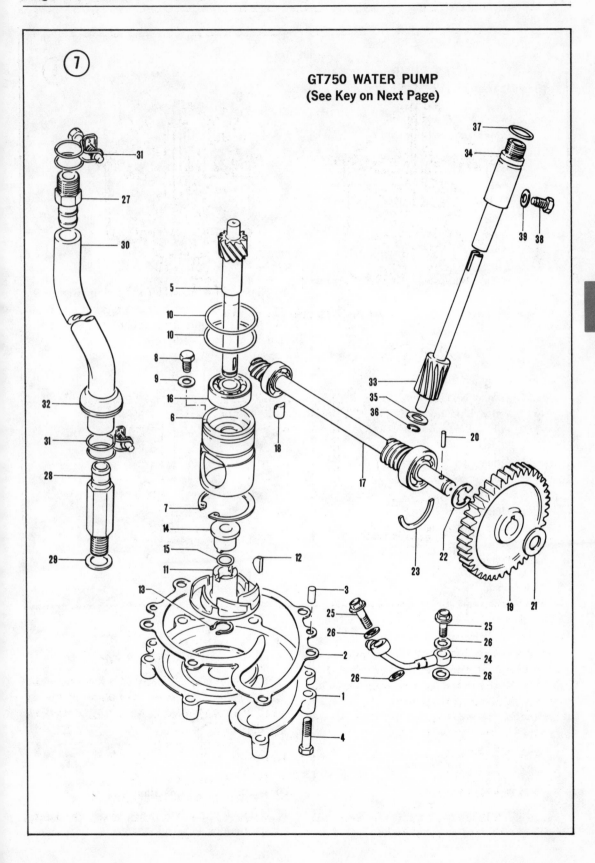

GT750 WATER PUMP
(See Key on Next Page)

GT750 WATER PUMP
(See Diagram on Previous Page)

1. Water pump case
2. Water pump case gasket
3. Dowel pin
4. Bolt
5. Water pump driven shaft
6. Pump driven shaft holder
7. Circlip
8. Water pump holder bolt
9. Washer
10. O-ring
11. Water pump impeller
12. Key
13. Circlip
14. Water pump sealing seat
15. O-ring
16. Bearing
17. Water pump drive shaft
18. Pump drive shaft pin
19. Water pump driven gear
20. Pump driven gear pin
21. Washer
22. E-ring
23. Pump drive shaft ring
24. Air breather pipe
25. Union bolt
26. Union bolt gasket
27. Water by-pass hose No. 1 union
28. Water by-pass hose No. 2 union
29. Union gasket
30. Water by-pass hose
31. Water by-pass hose clamp
32. Grommet
33. Tachometer driven gear
34. Tachometer driven gear sleeve
35. Thrust washer
36. Circlip
37. O-ring
38. Driven gear sleeve bolt
39. Washer

4. Remove the impeller after removing its snap ring (**Figure 8**).

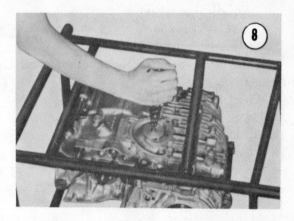

5. Remove pump holder snap ring (**Figure 9**), then wrap the pump shaft in a rag and pull it out with pliers (**Figure 10**). Be sure that the pump shaft is not damaged during this step.

Disassembly and Inspection

1. Heat the pump holder and shaft assembly to approximately 165-185 degrees F (75-85 de

grees C), then pull the shaft from the pump holder.

> NOTE: *Do not attempt to remove the seals from the pump holder. Replace the pump holder if these seals are damaged.*

2. Check the bearing for roughness or excessive end play.

3. Remove any rust or corrosion from the pump shaft, using emery paper.

4. Check the impeller for bent or broken blades.

5. Be sure that the seal seat is not worn excessively. Replace the pump holder and seal seat if this condition exists.

6. Check the O-rings for wear or damage.

7. Check the drive gears and bearings for wear or roughness.

8. Check the outer surface and the circumference of the impeller for evidence of rubbing against the crankcase or pump cover. There should be 0.02 to 0.06 inch (0.5 to 1.5 millimeter) gap between the impeller and crankcase.

Reassembly

Reverse the disassembly procedure to reassemble the water pump. Observe the following points:

1. Lubricate the outside of the water pump holder with oil before installation.

2. Be sure that the hole in the pump holder aligns with the hole in the crankcase. Rotate the holder slightly each way so that the crankcase bolt engages the notch in the pump holder.

3. Install the impeller, then install its snap ring. Be sure that there is 0.06 inch (1.5 millimeters) clearance between the impeller and crankcase.

4. Apply gasket cement to both sides of the gasket before installing the pump cover.

COOLING SYSTEM MAINTENANCE

Because of the special nature of a liquid cooling system, certain cautions must be observed, and certain maintenance operations performed periodically.

Coolant Solution

As a general rule, the cooling system should be kept filled with a mixture of half distilled water and half permanent type (ethylene glycol) antifreeze solution. Antifreeze is necessary, not only for protection from freezing, but also because it contains corrosion inhibitors. It also acts as a water pump lubricant and serves to raise the boiling point of the coolant solution (**Figure 11**). For these reasons, coolant solutions with less than 30 percent antifreeze are not recommended at any time.

Ordinary tap water is usually not suitable for use. Most tap water contains minerals which may cause corrosion in the engine and radiator. Always use distilled water when making up new coolant solution. Distilled water is available at almost any supermarket. It is sold for use in steam irons.

Table 3 lists approximate proportions of distilled water and anti-freeze required for refill after draining. When adding a small amount to make up for normal loss, use distilled water. If more than a little is needed, use a mixture of water and anti-freeze.

Always check coolant level before starting the engine. With the engine cold, coolant level should be 0.2 to 0.6 inch (5 to 15 millimeters) from the bottom of the reservoir (**Figure 12**).

Table 3   ENGINE COOLANT

Concentration (percent)	Antifreeze Quarts	(Liters)	Distilled Water Quarts	(Liters)	Protects to Degrees F	(Degrees C)
30	1.40	(1.35)	3.30	(3.15)	14	(−10)
40	1.90	(1.80)	2.90	(2.70)	−4	(−20)
50	2.40	(2.25)	2.40	(2.25)	−24	(−31)
60	2.90	(2.70)	1.90	(1.80)	−58	(−50)

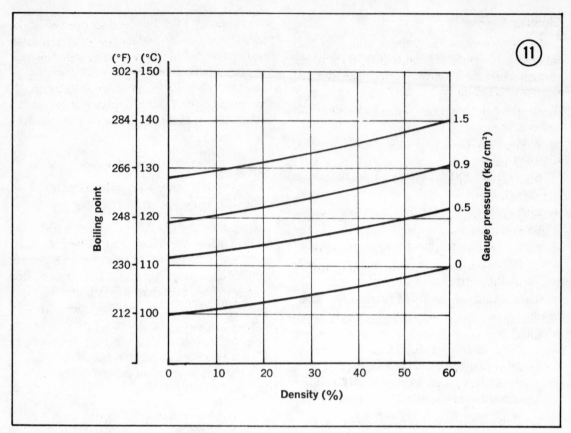

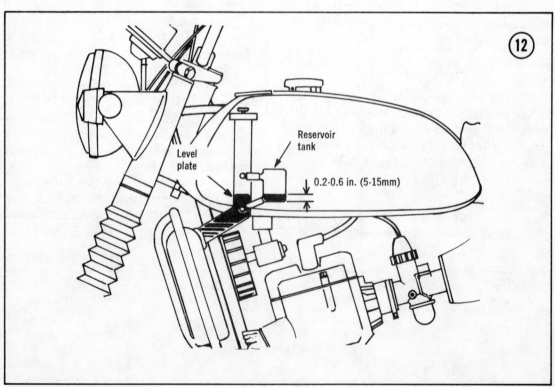

Flushing System

Every two years or 20,000 miles (35,000 kilometers), whichever comes first, the cooling system must be drained, flushed, and refilled with fresh solution.

1. Remove the crankcase water drain plug and radiator cap.

2. Replace the drain plug, then refill the system with tap water.

3. Run the engine until it is at normal operating temperature.

4. Repeat Steps 1, 2, and 3 until the drained water is colorless.

5. Replace the drain plug and tighten it securely.

6. Fill the system with antifreeze and distilled water mixture.

7. Add approximately 2⅓ ounces (70 cubic centimeters) liquid stop-leak to the coolant solution.

CAUTION

Be sure that the stop-leak used is compatible with permanent type antifreeze and aluminum engines.

8. Run the engine until normal operating temperature is reached, then check for leaks.

9. Check and adjust coolant level after the engine has cooled.

FAN CIRCUIT

The fan is controlled by a thermoswitch. Whenever coolant temperature rises to 221 degrees F (105 degrees C), the fan begins to operate. As coolant temperature drops to about 212 degrees F (100 degrees C), the fan stops.

To test the fan circuit, turn the ignition switch on, then disconnect the brown wire from the thermoswitch on the cylinder head. The fan should operate with the wire disconnected. If the fan does not operate, test the fan motor and relay by disconnecting the brown/white wire from the fan, then applying battery power to that wire. If the motor then works, the relay is defective. If the motor doesn't work, replace or repair the motor.

TROUBLESHOOTING

Table 4 lists symptoms, probable causes, and remedies for possible cooling system problems.

Table 4   TROUBLESHOOTING

Overheating	
a. Insufficient coolant	Replenish solution
b. Clogged system	Clean
c. Incorrect ignition timing	Adjust
d. Sticking thermostat	Replace
e. Defective pump	Replace
f. Dragging brakes	Adjust
g. Fan inoperative	Repair
Overcooling	
a. Defective thermostat	Replace
b. Cold weather	Cover radiator
Coolant loss	
a. Leaking radiator	Repair
b. Loose hoses	Tighten clamps
c. Leaking pump cover	Repair or replace
d. Defective head gasket	Replace
e. Warped cylinder head	Resurface or replace
f. Cracked cylinder head	Replace
g. Cracked cylinder block	Replace
h. Defective pressure cap	Replace
Noise	
a. Defective water pump	Replace
b. Loose or bent impeller	Replace

4

CHAPTER FIVE

ELECTRICAL SYSTEM

This chapter discusses operating principles and troubleshooting procedures for Suzuki ignition, charging, starting, signal, and lighting systems. All Suzuki 3-cylinder machines are equipped with alternators as the source of electrical system power.

IGNITION SYSTEM

All models are equipped with battery ignition systems. This system operates in a manner similar to that of a conventional automobile.

Operation

Figure 1 is a simplified diagram of the ignition system used on these machines. Note that the system is shown for a single cylinder only; all components except the battery, fuse, and ignition switch are duplicated for the other cylinders.

When the breaker points are closed, current flows from the battery through the primary winding of the ignition coil, thereby building a magnetic field around the coil. The breaker cam rotates with the crankshaft and is so adjusted that the breaker points open as the piston reaches the firing position.

As the points open, the magnetic field collapses. When the field collapses, a very high voltage (up to approximately 15,000 volts) is induced in the secondary winding of the ignition coil. This high voltage is sufficient to jump the gap at the spark plug.

The condenser assists the coil in its job of developing high voltage, and also serves to protect the breaker points. Inductance of the ignition coil primary tends to keep a surge of current flowing through the circuit even after the points have started to open. The condenser stores this surge and thus prevents arcing at the points.

Troubleshooting

Ignition system problems can be classified as no spark, weak spark, or improperly timed spark. These conditions can affect any or all cylinders of a multicylinder engine. **Table 1** lists common causes and remedies for ignition system malfunction.

If the problem is no spark at any cylinder, it is almost certainly because current is not reaching any coil. Since the only current is through the battery connections and main switch, the defect will be easy to locate.

Ignition failures confined to one cylinder are also easy to isolate.

1. Rotate the engine until the points associated with the affected cylinder are closed.

2. Disconnect the high voltage lead from the affected spark plug and hold it ¼ in. away from

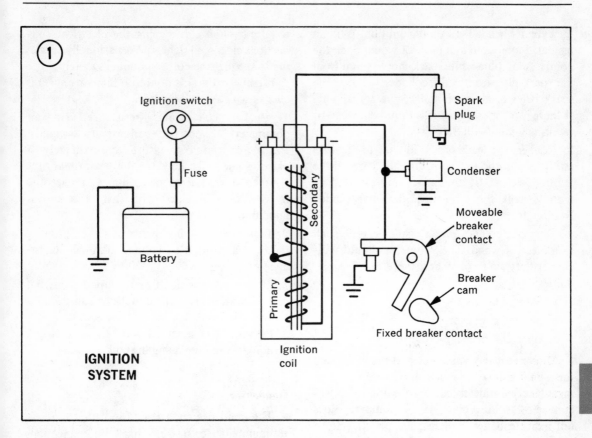

① IGNITION SYSTEM

Ignition switch

Spark plug

Fuse

+ −

Secondary

Condenser

Moveable breaker contact

Breaker cam

Battery

Primary

Fixed breaker contact

Ignition coil

5

Table 1   IGNITION SYSTEM TROUBLESHOOTING

Symptom	Probable Cause	Remedy
No spark, or weak spark, all cylinders	Discharged battery	Charge battery
	Defective fuse	Replace
	Defective main switch	Replace
	Loose or corroded connections	Clean and tighten
	Broken wire	Repair
No spark, or weak spark, one cylinder only	Incorrect point gap	Reset points. Be sure to readjust ignition timing
	Dirty or oily points	Clean points
	Spark plug lead damaged	Replace wire
	Broken primary wire	Repair wire
	Open winding in coil	Replace coil
	Shorted winding in coil	Replace coil
	Defective condenser	Replace condenser
Misfires	Dirty spark plugs	Clean or replace plug
	Spark plug is too hot	Replace with colder plug
	Spark plug is too cold	Replace with hotter plug
	Spring on ignition points is weak	Replace points, reset timing
	Incorrect timing	Adjust timing

the cylinder head. Turn on the ignition. With an insulated tool, such as a piece of wood, open the points. A fat, blue-white spark should jump from the spark plug lead to the cylinder head. If the spark is good, clean or replace the spark plug. If there is no spark, or if it is thin, yellowish, or weak, continue with Step 3.

3. Connect the leads of a voltmeter to the wire on the points and to a good ground. Turn on the ignition switch. If the meter indicates more than ⅛ volt, the problem is defective points. Replace them.

4. Open the points with an insulated tool, such as a piece of wood. The voltmeter should indicate battery voltage. If not, there are 3 possibilities:

   a. Shorted points

   b. Shorted condenser

   c. Open coil primary circuit

5. Disconnect the condenser and the wire from the points. Connect the ungrounded (positive on most bikes) voltmeter lead to the wire which was connected to the points. If the voltmeter does not indicate battery voltage, the problem is an open coil primary circuit. Replace the suspected coil with a known good one. You may borrow one from another cylinder. If that coil doesn't work, the problem is in the primary wiring.

6. If the voltmeter indicates battery voltage in Step 5, the coil primary circuit is OK. Connect the positive voltmeter lead to the wire which goes from the coil to the points. Block the points open with a business card or similar piece of cardboard. Connect the negative voltmeter lead to the movable point. If the voltmeter indicates any voltage, the points are shorted and must be replaced.

7. If the foregoing checks are satisfactory, the problem is in the coil or condenser. Substitute each of these separately with a known good one from another cylinder to determine which is defective.

Ignition Coil

The ignition coil is a form of transformer which develops the high voltage required to jump the spark plug gap. The only maintenance required is that of keeping the electrical connections clean and tight, and occasionally checking to see that the coil is mounted securely.

If coil condition is doubtful, there are several checks which may be made.

1. Measure coil primary resistance, using an ohmmeter, between both coil primary terminals. Resistance should measure approximately 5 ohms. Some coils, however, have a primary resistance of less than one ohm. Compare the measurement obtained with that of a known good one.

2. Measure resistance between either primary terminal and the high voltage terminal. Resistance range should be 10,000 to 25,000 ohms.

3. If these checks don't reveal any defects, but coil condition is still doubtful, substitute a known good one.

Be sure to connect all wires to their proper terminals when replacing the coil.

Condenser

The condenser is a sealed unit that requires no maintenance. Be sure that both connections are clean and tight.

Two tests can be made on the condenser. Measure condenser capacity with a condenser tester. Capacity should be 0.16 to 0.20 microfarad. The other test is insulation resistance, which should not be less than 5 megohms, measured between the condenser pigtail and case.

In the event that no test equipment is available, a quick test of the condenser may be made by connecting the condenser case to the negative terminal of a 12-volt battery, and the positive lead to the positive battery terminal. Allow the condenser to charge for a few seconds, then quickly disconnect the battery and touch the condenser pigtail to the condenser case. If you observe a spark as the pigtail touches the case, you may assume that the condenser is OK.

Arcing between the breaker points is a common symptom of condenser failure.

Breaker Points

Refer to Chapter Two for details of breaker point service.

ALTERNATOR

An alternator is a form of electrical generator in which a magnetized field called a rotor, revolves within a set of stationary coils called a stator. As the rotor revolves, alternating current is induced in the stator. Stator current is then rectified and used to operate electrical accessories and for charging the battery.

The output from the alternator is controlled by a voltage regulator, which performs its function by controlling the amount of field current to the alternator rotor.

Suzuki machines are equipped with either Denso (**Figure 2**) or Kokusan (**Figure 3**) alternators. Service procedures for the 2 types are similar. Differences will be pointed out where they exist. Charging system connections (**Figure 4**) are the same for both systems.

If alternator or regulator problems are suspected, as in the case of a chronically undercharged battery or dim headlights, check alternator output voltage.

1. Connect a 0-20 DC voltmeter across the battery terminals (**Figure 5**). Be sure to connect the positive voltmeter lead to the positive battery terminal, and the negative voltmeter lead to the negative battery terminal.

2. Start the engine and run it at 2,000 to 3,000 rpm. If the voltmeter indicates 13.5 to 14.5 volts, you may assume that the alternator and regulator are OK.

3. If the voltmeter does not indicate 13.5 to 14.5 volts, further checking will be required. Trouble may lie in the alternator, regulator, or wiring. Proceed with Steps 4 through 8.

4. Measure field winding resistance between both alternator slip rings. If resistance is not approximately as specified, replace the rotor.

Denso rotor	10-12 ohms
Kokusan rotor	4-5 ohms

5. Measure insulation resistance of the field winding. Set the ohmmeter to its highest range, then measure resistance between either slip ring and the rotor shaft. Insulation resistance must be essentially infinite.

6. Check the alternator brushes (**Figure 6**) for wear. Replace Denso brushes when they are worn to 0.28 in. (7mm). Kokusan brushes should be replaced when they are worn to the limit mark on the brush. On GT750 models, replace brushes when they are worn to 0.22 in. (5.5mm).

7. Check for continuity between each pair of yellow wires coming from the alternator stator.

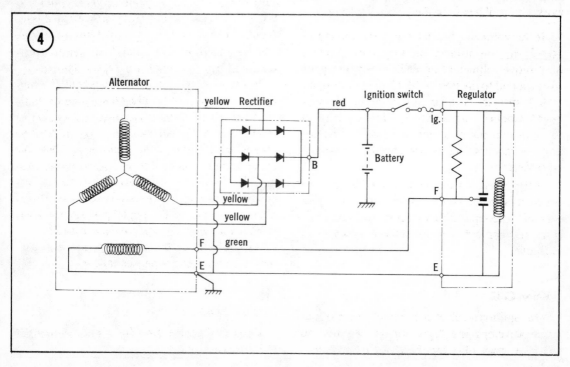

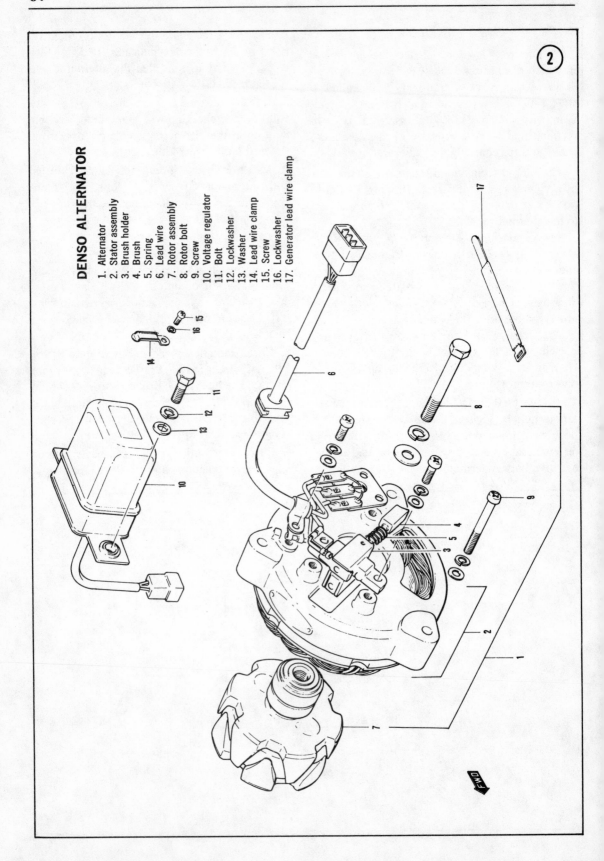

DENSO ALTERNATOR

1. Alternator
2. Stator assembly
3. Brush holder
4. Brush
5. Spring
6. Lead wire
7. Rotor assembly
8. Rotor bolt
9. Screw
10. Voltage regulator
11. Bolt
12. Lockwasher
13. Washer
14. Lead wire clamp
15. Screw
16. Lockwasher
17. Generator lead wire clamp

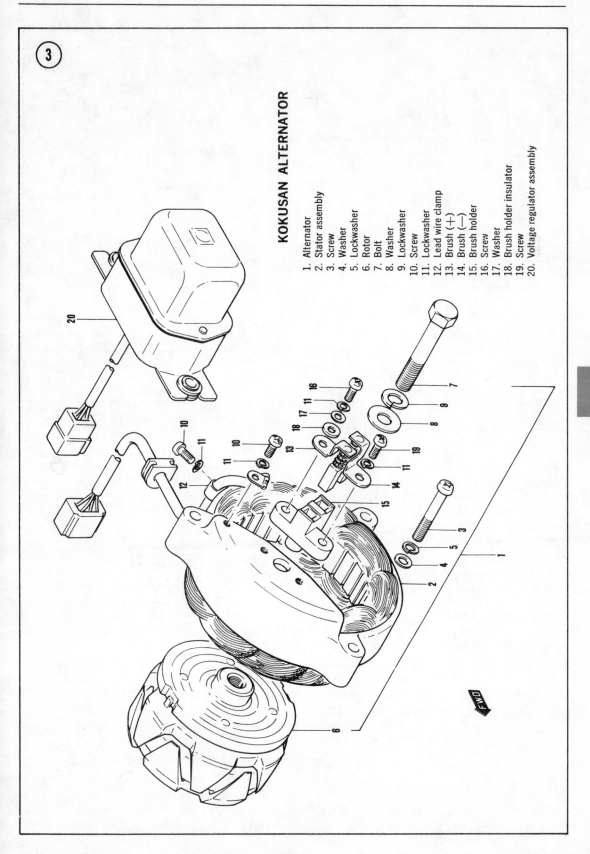

KOKUSAN ALTERNATOR

1. Alternator
2. Stator assembly
3. Screw
4. Washer
5. Lockwasher
6. Rotor
7. Bolt
8. Washer
9. Lockwasher
10. Screw
11. Lockwasher
12. Lead wire clamp
13. Brush (+)
14. Brush (−)
15. Brush holder
16. Screw
17. Washer
18. Brush holder insulator
19. Screw
20. Voltage regulator assembly

5

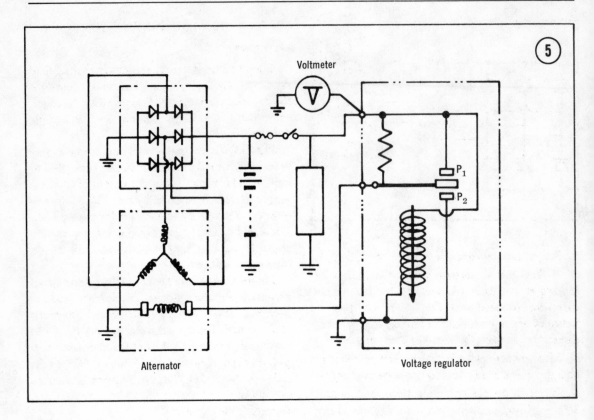

Voltmeter

Alternator   Voltage regulator

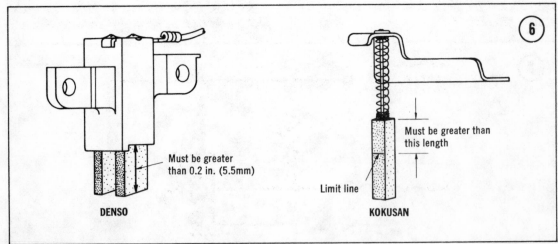

Must be greater
than 0.2 in. (5.5mm)

DENSO

Must be greater than
this length

Limit line

KOKUSAN

8. Set the ohmmeter to its highest range, then measure insulation resistance between the stator housing and any of the 3 yellow leads. Insulation resistance must be essentially infinite.

RECTIFIER

The rectifier assembly serves 2 purposes. It converts alternating current produce by the al-ternator into direct current which is used to charge the battery. It also prevents discharge of the battery through the alternator when the engine isn't running, or at other times when alternator output voltage is less than battery voltage.

The rectifier assembly has 3 yellow leads, one red lead, and one black/white lead (**Figure 7**).

1. Measure resistance between each yellow lead and the red lead. Record each measurement.

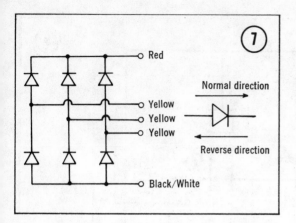

2. Reverse ohmmeter leads and repeat Step 1.

3. If each pair of measurements was essentially infinite in one direction and low in the reverse direction, proceed with Step 4. If any pair of measurements was either high or low in both directions, replace the rectifier assembly.

4. Measure resistance between each yellow lead and the black lead. Record each measurement.

5. Reverse the meter connections and repeat Step 4. If any pair of measurements was either high or low in both directions, replace the rectifier assembly.

VOLTAGE REGULATOR

Operation

Suzuki alternators use separately excited field windings. As engine speed increases, alternator output tends to increase. It is possible, however, to control alternator output by controlling field current.

Figure 8 illustrates the situation at low engine speeds. Rectified alternator output is applied to coil "B". However, since the output is low, the magnetic field developed by coil "B" is too low to open contacts P_1 and P_0. Under these conditions, field current is supplied by the battery through the ignition switch, and is at its maximum value.

Figure 9 illustrates the circuit as engine speed increases. As alternator output voltage tends to increase, coil "B" generates more magnetic force, which breaks contacts P_1 and P_0. Field current is then supplied from the alternator output through resistor "C". Resistor "C" limits field current, and thereby reduces alternator output so that contacts C_1 and C_0 again close, repeating the cycle.

At high engine speeds and light electrical loads, action of the upper and center contacts is

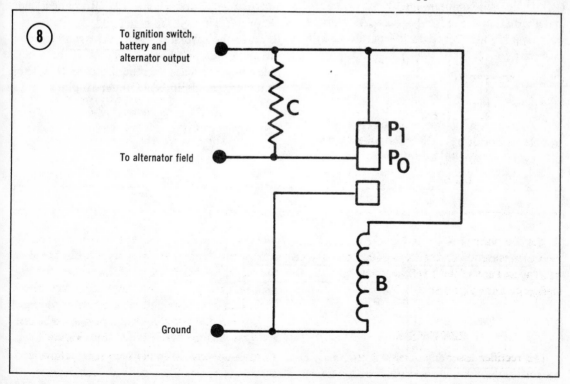

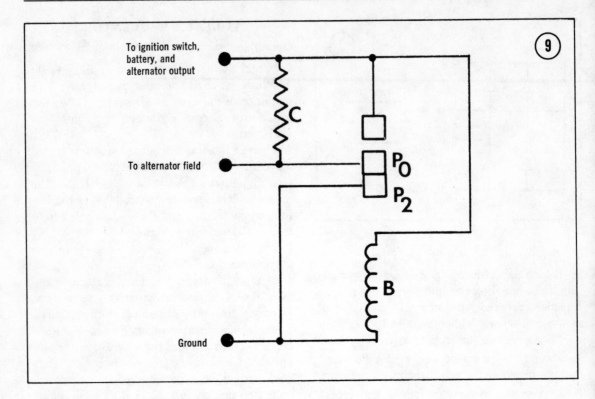

insufficient to control alternator output. As output voltage continues to rise, coil "B" pulls the movable contact (P_0) down to the lower contact (P_2). Under this condition the field is grounded, and alternator output drops to zero. As is drops, the movable and lower contacts separate, and the cycle repeats.

Regulator Testing

The most common causes of voltage regulator trouble are open wires or short circuits. To check the regulator, proceed as follows.

1. Remove the regulator.

2. Check for continuity between the green and orange wires, and also between the black/white and orange wires (**Figure 10**). Reconnect the ohmmeter between the green and orange leads. Remove the regulator cover, then gently press the armature (1 in **Figure 11**) so that the movable contact touches the other fixed contact. The ohmmeter should indicate about 10 ohms.

NOTE: *The regulator cover is sealed to prevent entry of dirt and moisture. Do not remove the regulator cover unless it is necessary to do so.*

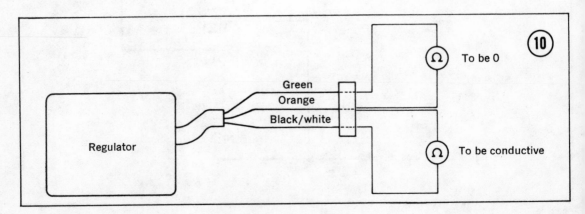

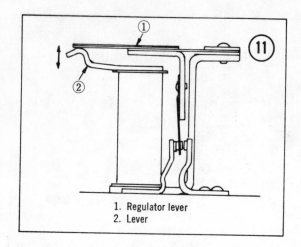

1. Regulator lever
2. Lever

2. Connect a voltmeter of known accuracy to measure system voltage (Figure 4).

3. Start the engine and run it at approximately 3,000 rpm. Note the voltmeter indication.

4. Bend the adjustment arm on Denso regulators, or turn the screw on Kokusan regulators (**Figure 12**) until the voltmeter indicates 14.0 ± 0.5 volts.

5. Turn off the ignition and replace the cover.

6. Check adjustment with cover installed.

3. Connect a voltmeter across the battery terminals. Reconnect the regulator.

4. Start the engine and run it at 3,000 rpm. If measured voltage is 14.0 ± 0.5 the regulator is OK. Adjust or replace the regulator if regulated voltage is not within those limits.

NOTE: *Denso and Kokusan r gulators are interchangeable.*

Voltage Regulator Adjustment

Do not attempt to adjust the regulator unless it has first been determined that all other parts of the charging system are in good condition.

1. With the engine not running, and the ignition switch off, remove the regulator cover.

ELECTRIC STARTER

Models GT550 and GT750 are equipped with electric self-starters. Starting motors are supplied by 2 different manufacturers, Denso and Kokusan, so it is important to specify the make of motor when ordering replacement parts. Service procedures are similar; differences will be pointed out where they exist.

Starter Operation

Figure 13 illustrates a typical starter motor circuit. When the rider presses the engine starter button, current flows from the battery through the coil of the starter relay, causing the relay armature to connect terminals "M" and "B". Current then flows directly from the battery to the starter motor. **Figure 14** is a pictorial diagram of the system connections.

5

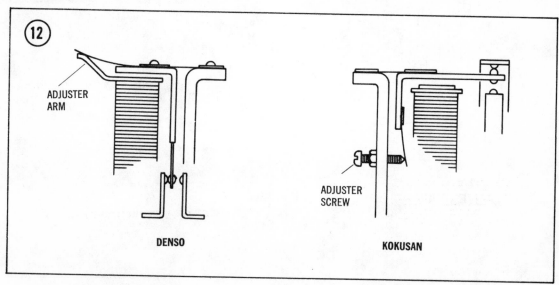

ADJUSTER ARM

DENSO

ADJUSTER SCREW

KOKUSAN

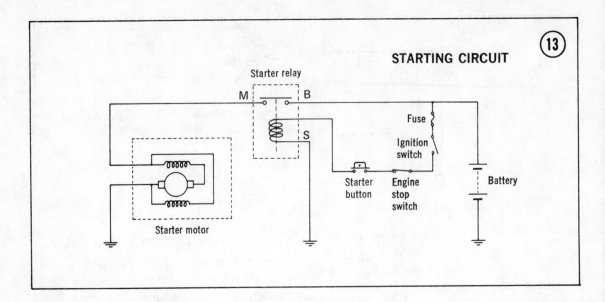

STARTING CIRCUIT ⑬

Figure 15 illustrates a typical starter drive train. When the starter turns, torque is transmitted through, and multiplied by, the idler gear and starter clutch gear. The starter clutch will transmit torque in only one direction. When the engine starts, the outer race, connected to the clutch housing, overruns the inner race and disconnects the drive. Note that since the starter drives the clutch housing, the engine may be started with the transmission in gear if the clutch is released.

Starter Disassembly

Figures 16 and 17 are exploded views of Denso and Kokusan starting motors; refer to the

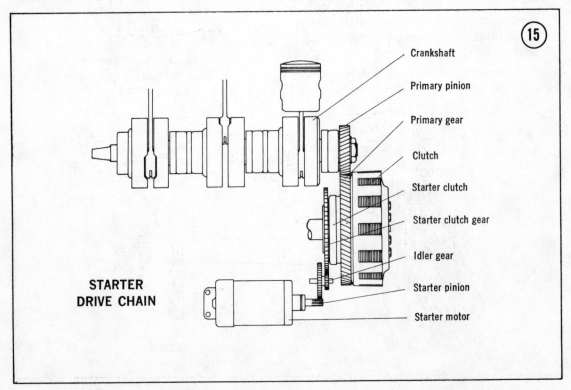

STARTER DRIVE CHAIN

Crankshaft
Primary pinion
Primary gear
Clutch
Starter clutch
Starter clutch gear
Idler gear
Starter pinion
Starter motor

⑮

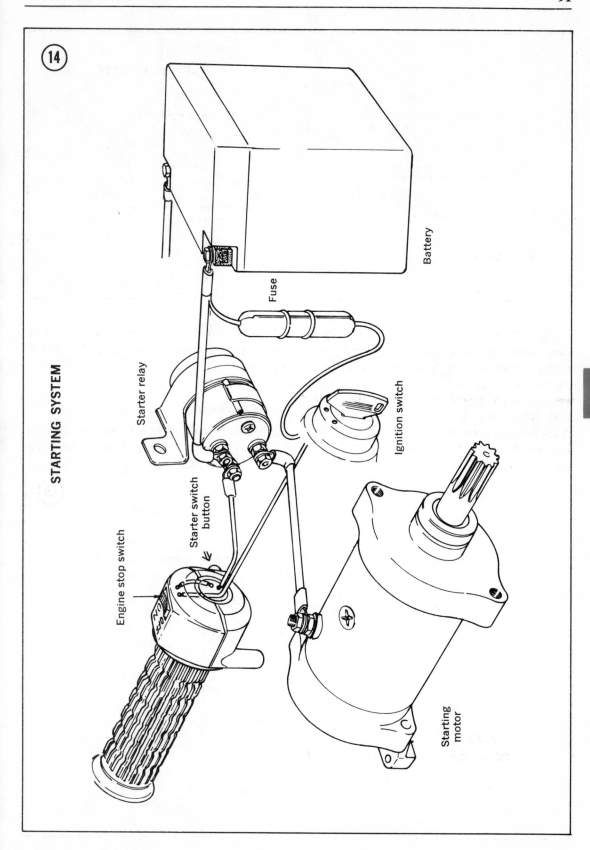

STARTING SYSTEM

14

Battery

Fuse

Starter relay

Ignition switch

Engine stop switch

Starter switch button

Starting motor

5

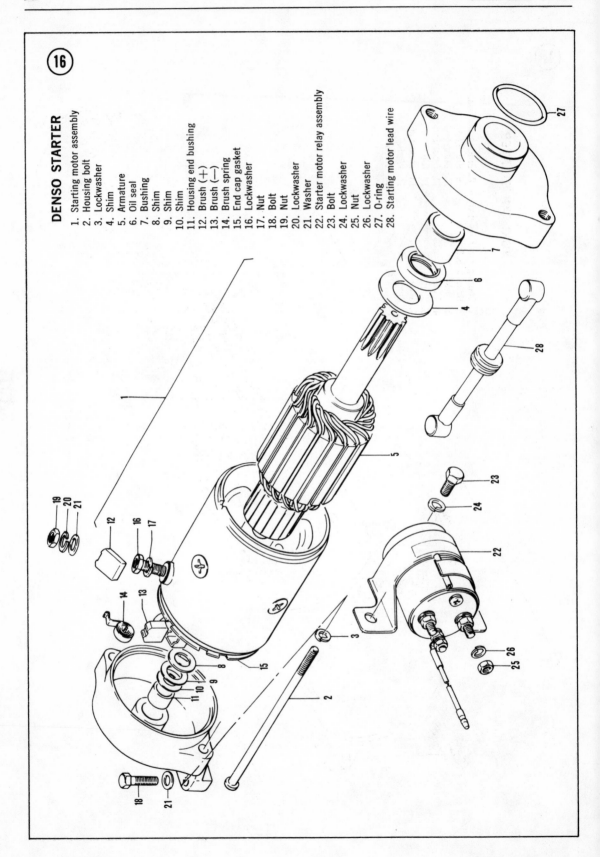

16

DENSO STARTER

1. Starting motor assembly
2. Housing bolt
3. Lockwasher
4. Shim
5. Armature
6. Oil seal
7. Bushing
8. Shim
9. Shim
10. Shim
11. Housing end bushing
12. Brush (+)
13. Brush (−)
14. Brush spring
15. End cap gasket
16. Lockwasher
17. Nut
18. Bolt
19. Nut
20. Lockwasher
21. Washer
22. Starter motor relay assembly
23. Bolt
24. Lockwasher
25. Nut
26. Lockwasher
27. O-ring
28. Starting motor lead wire

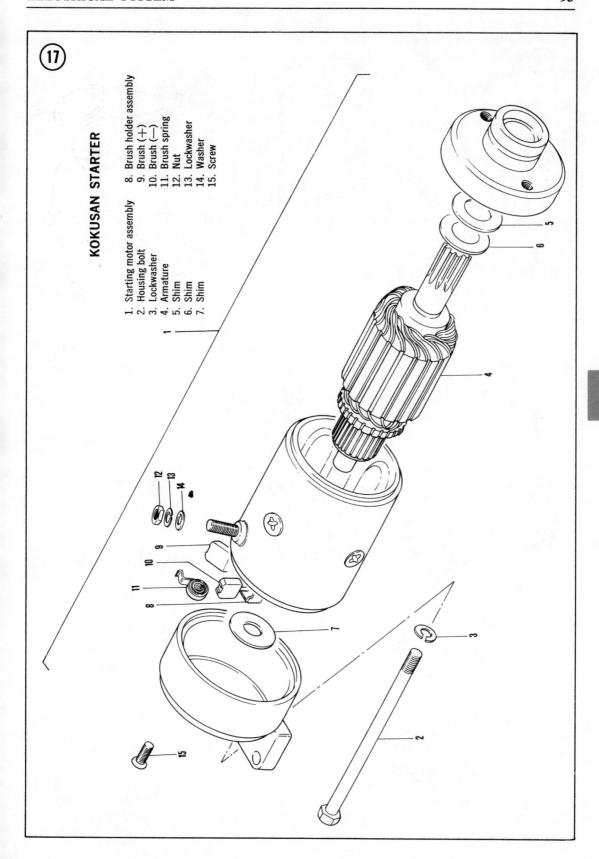

KOKUSAN STARTER

1. Starting motor assembly
2. Housing bolt
3. Lockwasher
4. Armature
5. Shim
6. Shim
7. Shim
8. Brush holder assembly
9. Brush (+)
10. Brush (−)
11. Brush spring
12. Nut
13. Lockwasher
14. Washer
15. Screw

5

applicable illustration during disassembly and reassembly. To disassemble the starting motor, proceed as follows.

1. Remove both thru-bolts, commutator end frame, bolts, brushes, shims, and thrust washers. Note locations of all small parts as they are removed.

2. Press out bushings from both end frames.

3. Reassembly is the reverse of disassembly. Pay particular attention to the following points.

   a. Apply a small amount of multipurpose grease to both armature bushings.

   b. Install armature brushes into the brush holders after armature is installed.

   c. Be sure that all shims and thrust washers are positioned correctly.

   d. Be sure that the shaft turns freely.

Starting Motor Overhaul

1. Measure clearance between each bushing and the armature shaft. Replace bushings if clearance exceeds 0.008 in. (0.2mm).

2. Examine the commutator for rough, burned, or scored segments, and for possible signs of overheating or thrown solder.

3. Mount the armature in a lathe, V-blocks, or other suitable centering device and measure the commutator for runout. If runout exceeds 0.012 in. (0.3mm) turn it down, but do not take off so much that overall commutator diameter is less than 1.045 in. (26.5mm).

4. After turning, undercut the mica insulators between commutator segments to 0.020-0.030 in. (0.5-0.8mm). If commutator turning was not required, be sure that the mica insulators are undercut at least 0.012 in. (0.3mm), as shown in **Figure 18**. A broken hacksaw blade is a suitable tool for undercutting the mica. Be sure to clean each slot thoroughly.

5. Using an ohmmeter or armature growler, test each commutator segment to be sure that it is not shorted to ground. Replace the armature if any short exists. Do not connect either test probe to the bearing surfaces of the shaft.

6. Using an armature growler, test for armature coil shorts. Follow the manufacturer's instructions on the test equipment.

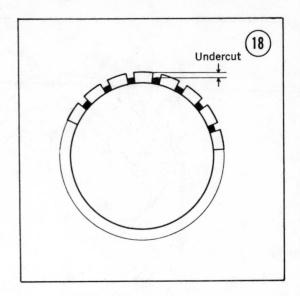

Undercut

7. Using an ohmmeter or armature tester, check for open windings in the armature (**Figure 19**).

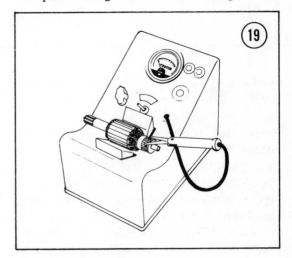

8. With the armature removed, test the shunt field coils by connecting the motorcycle battery between the starter terminal and the starter housing as shown in **Figure 20**. Insert a screwdriver into the motor housing. If the screwdriver is drawn to coils "A" and "C", the shunt field coils are not open. Do not leave the battery connected any longer than is necessary to make this test.

9. Disconnect the shunt field coil wire at the ground brush. Then with an ohmmeter set to its highest range, check for continuity between the starter terminal and ground. If the ohmmeter

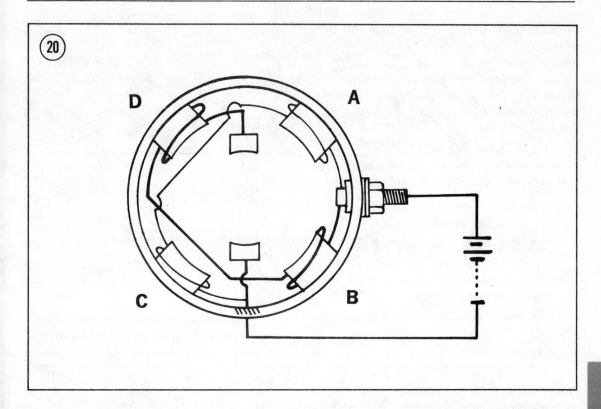

indicates anything other than an open circuit, replace the shunt field coils. Shunt field coil resistance, measured between the starter terminal and the grounded brush, should be approximately 2.5 ohms.

10. Check series field coils by connecting the motorcycle battery between both brushes, as shown in **Figure 21**. Then again insert a screwdriver into the motor housing. The screwdriver should be attracted to the *shunt* coils ("A" and "C"). Do not leave the battery connected any longer than is necessary to make this test.

11. Disconnect the shunt coil wire at the starter terminal. With an ohmmeter set to its highest range, measure between the starter terminal and the motor housing. If the ohmmeter indicates anything other than an open circuit, replace the series field coil.

12. With the ohmmeter set to its highest range, check for any short circuit between the insulated starter brush and ground. Repair or replace the brush holder if any short circuit exists.

13. Examine both starter brushes. Replace them when they are worn to the limits shown in **Figure 22**.

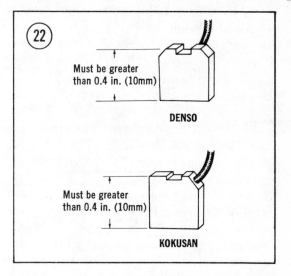

14. Upon reassembly, check brush spring tension. If tension is less than 0.85 pound (600 grams), replace the springs.

STARTER RELAY

The starter relay controls operating current to the starter motor. When the starter button is pressed, the relay coil is energized, closing the

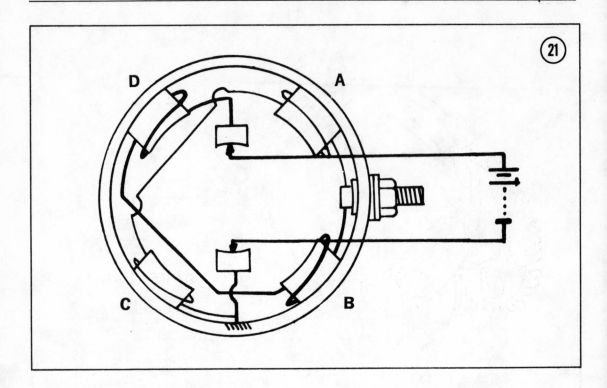

relay contacts. Current then flows from the battery, through the relay contacts, and finally through the starting motor.

To check the starter relay, momentarily connect the battery as shown in **Figure 23**. The relay should click as the battery is connected. Then remove the relay cover and check the contacts for burrs or roughness. Dress the contacts, if necessary, with a fine file.

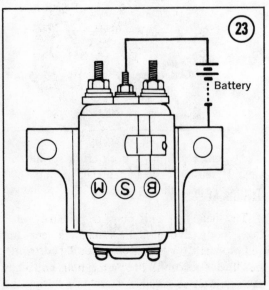

STARTER CLUTCH

The starter clutch transmits torque from the starter to the engine, but releases whenever the engine overruns the starter. **Figure 24** is a simplified drawing of the starter clutch mechanism.

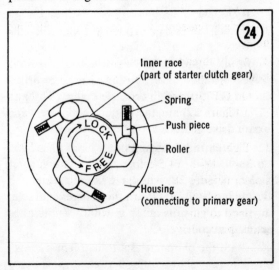

Figures 25 and 26 are exploded views of starter clutches for models GT550 and GT750, respectively. Refer to the appropriate illustration during disassembly and reassembly.

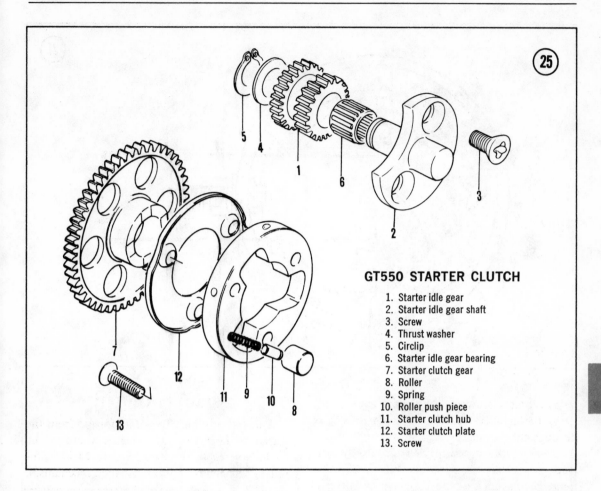

GT550 STARTER CLUTCH

1. Starter idle gear
2. Starter idle gear shaft
3. Screw
4. Thrust washer
5. Circlip
6. Starter idle gear bearing
7. Starter clutch gear
8. Roller
9. Spring
10. Roller push piece
11. Starter clutch hub
12. Starter clutch plate
13. Screw

During reassembly, observe the following notes.

1. Apply thread lock cement to each assembly bolt or screw.

2. On GT750 models, be sure that punch mark (1 in **Figure 27**) aligns with pin (2) on the water pump drive gear.

3. Tighten the retaining nut on model GT750 to 33-40 ft.-lb. (4.5-5.5 mkg). A starter clutch holder (**Figure 28**) will make the job easier.

4. On model GT750, turn the breaker cam shaft by hand to align its cutaway with the pin on the water pump drive gear (**Figure 29**).

1. Punch mark 2. Pin

LIGHTS

Machines which are intended to be ridden on public streets are equipped with lights. Check them periodically to be sure that they are working properly.

Headlight

The headlight unit consists primarily of a lamp body, a dual-filament bulb, a lens and reflector unit, a rim, and a socket. To adjust the headlight, loosen the 2 mounting bolts and move the assembly as required.

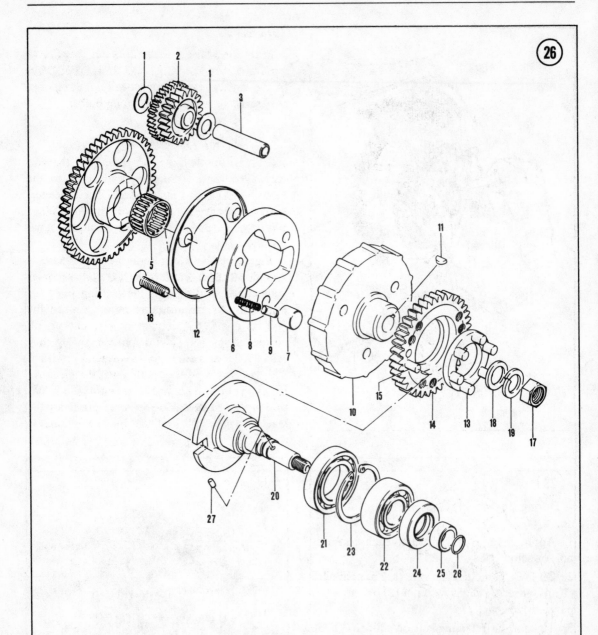

GT750 STARTER CLUTCH

1. Starter idle gear washer
2. Starter idle gear
3. Idle gear pin
4. Starter clutch gear
5. Starter clutch bearing
6. Starter clutch hub
7. Roller
8. Starter clutch spring
9. Push piece

10. Starter clutch housing
11. Key
12. Starter clutch plate
13. Breaker cam shaft rubber
14. Water pump drive gear
15. Breaker cam shaft drive pin
16. Screw
17. Nut
18. Washer

19. Lockwasher
20. Breaker cam shaft
21. Breaker cam shaft bearing
22. Bearing
23. Circlip
24. Oil seal
25. Spacer
26. O-ring
27. Dowel pin

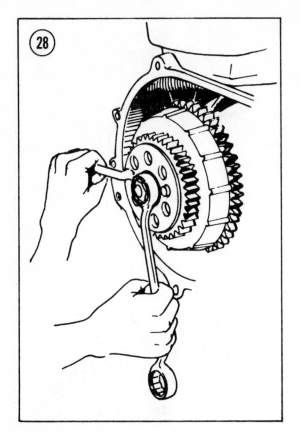

Turn Signals

If any turn signal bulb burns out, be sure to replace it with the same type. Improper action of the flasher relay, or even failure to operate may result from use of the wrong bulbs.

HORN

Current for the horn is supplied by the battery. One horn terminal is connected to the battery through the main switch. The other terminal is connected to the horn button. When the rider presses the button, current flows through the horn.

Figure 30 illustrates horn operation. As current flows through the coil, the core becomes magnetized, and attracts the moving plate, or armature. As the armature moves toward the coil, it opens the contact points, cutting off current to the coil. The diaphragm spring then returns the armature to its original position. This process repeats rapidly until the rider releases the horn button. The action of the armature striking the end of the core produces the sound, which is amplified by the resonator diaphragm (**Figure 31**).

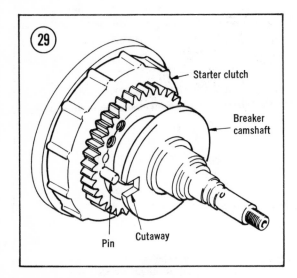

Starter clutch

Breaker camshaft

Pin   Cutaway

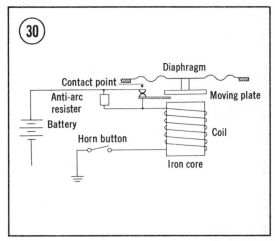

Diaphragm

Contact point

Anti-arc resister

Battery

Horn button

Moving plate

Coil

Iron core

Brake Light

The switch is actuated by the brake pedal. Adjust the switch so that the stoplight goes on just before braking action occurs. Move the switch body up or down as required for adjustment. Tighten the clamp nut after adjustment.

Horn tone may be adjusted by turning the adjuster screw in the back of the horn assembly. Loosen the locknut before adjustment, then be sure to retighten it after adjustment is complete.

The horn will not sound if its contact points are burned. Dress them if necessary, using a small point file or flex stone. Adjust the horn after dressing its contact points.

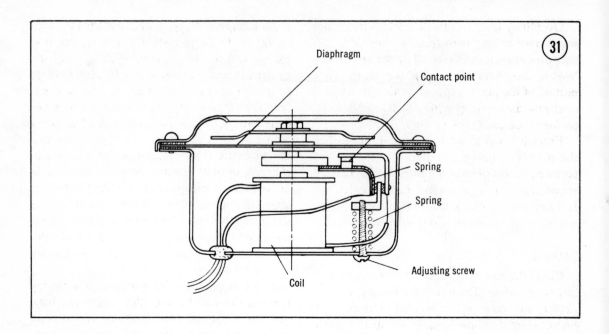

Diaphragm

Contact point

Spring

Spring

Adjusting screw

Coil

BATTERY

Suzuki motorcycles are equipped with lead-acid storage batteries, smaller in size but similar in construction to batteries used in automobiles.

WARNING
Read and thoroughly understand the section on safety precautions before doing any battery service.

Safety Precautions

When working with batteries, use extreme care to avoid spilling or splashing electrolyte. This electrolyte is sulphuric acid, which can destroy clothing and cause serious chemical burns. If any electrolyte is spilled or splashed on clothing or body, it should immediately be neutralized with a solution of baking soda and water, then flushed with plenty of clean water.

Electrolyte splashed into the eyes is extremely dangerous. Safety glasses should always be worn when working with batteries. If electrolyte is splashed into the eye, force the eye open, flood with cool clean water for about 5 minutes, and call a physician immediately.

If electrolyte is spilled or splashed onto painted or unpainted surfaces, it should be neutralized immediately with baking soda solution and then rinsed with clean water.

When batteries are being charged, highly explosive hydrogen gas forms in each cell. Some of this gas escapes through the filler openings and may form an explosive atmosphere around the battery. *This explosive atmosphere may exist for several hours.* Sparks, open flame, or a lighted cigarette can ignite this gas, causing an internal explosion and possible serious personal injury. The following precautions should be taken to prevent an explosion.

1. Do not smoke or permit any open flame near any battery being charged or which has been recently charged.

2. Do not disconnect live circuits at battery terminals, because a spark usually occurs when a live circuit is broken. Care must always be taken when connecting or disconnecting any battery charger; be sure its power switch is off before making or breaking connections. Poor connections are a common cause of electrical arcs which cause explosions.

Battery electrolyte level should be checked regularly, particularly during hot weather. Most batteries are marked with electrolyte level limit lines. Always maintain electrolyte level between the 2 lines, using distilled water as required for replenishment. Distilled water is available at almost every supermarket. It is sold for use in steam irons and is quite inexpensive.

Overfilling leads to loss of electrolyte, resulting in poor battery performance, short life, and excessive corrosion. Never allow the electrolyte level to drop below the top of the plates. That portion of the plates exposed to air may be permanently damaged, resulting in loss of battery performance and shortened life.

Excessive use of water is an indication that the battery is being overcharged. The 2 most common causes of overcharging are high battery temperature or high voltage regulator setting. It is advisable to check the voltage regulator, on machines so equipped, if this suitation exists.

Cleaning

Check the battery occasionally for presence of dirt or corrosion. The top of the battery, in particular, should be kept clean. Acid film and dirt permit current to flow between terminals, which will slowly discharge the battery.

For best results when cleaning, wash first with dilute ammonia or baking soda solution, then flush with plenty of clean water. Take care to keep filler plugs tight so that no cleaning solution enters the cells.

Battery Cables

To ensure good electrical contact, cables must be clean and tight on battery terminals. If the battery or cable terminals are corroded, the cables should be disconnected and cleaned separately with a wire brush and baking soda solution. After cleaning, apply a very thin coating of petroleum jelly to the battery terminals before installing the cables. After connecting the cables, apply a light coating to the connection. This procedure will help to prevent future corrosion.

Battery Charging

WARNING
Do not smoke or permit any open flame in any area where batteries are being charged, or immediately after charging. Highly explosive hydrogen gas is formed during the charging process. Be sure to re-read Safety Precautions *in the beginning of this section.*

Motorcycle batteries are not designed for high charge or discharge rates. For this reason, it is recommended that a motorcycle battery be charged at a rate not exceeding 10 percent of its ampere-hour capacity. That is, do not exceed 0.5 ampere charging rate for a 5 ampere-hour battery, or 1.5 amperes for a 15 ampere-hour battery. This charge rate should continue for 10 hours if the battery is completely discharged, or until specific gravity of each cell is up to 1.260-1.280, corrected for temperature. If after prolonged charging, specific gravity of one or more cells does not come up to at least 1.230, the battery will not perform as well as it should, but it may continue to provide satisfactory service for a time.

Some temperature rise is normal as a battery is being charged. Do not allow electrolyte temperature to exceed 110°F. Should temperature reach that figure, discontinue charging until the battery cools, then resume charging at a lower rate.

Testing State of Charge

A hydrometer is an inexpensive instrument which measures electrolyte specific gravity, which is directly related to state of charge.

To use a hydrometer, place its suction tube into the first filler opening, then draw in just enough electrolyte to lift its float. Hold the instrument in a vertical position, and read specific gravity on the float scale, where the float stem emerges from the electrolyte (**Figure 32**). Repeat this procedure for each battery cell.

Electrolyte specific gravity varies with temperature, so it is necessary to apply a temperature correction to the measurement so obtained. For each 10° that battery temperature exceeds 80°F, add 0.004 to the indicated specific gravity. Likewise, subtract 0.004 from the indicated value for each 10° that battery temperature is below 80°F.

Repeat this measurement for each battery cell. If there is more than 0.050 difference (50 points) between cells, battery condition is questionable.

State of charge of the battery may be determined from **Table 2**.

5

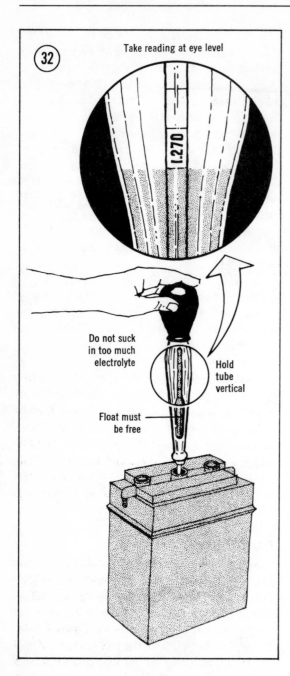

Take reading at eye level

1.270

Do not suck
in too much
electrolyte

Hold
tube
vertical

Float must
be free

Table 2   STATE OF CHARGE

Specific Gravity	State of Charge
1.110 - 1.130	Discharged
1.140 - 1.160	Almost discharged
1.170 - 1.190	One-quarter charged
1.200 - 1.220	One-half charged
1.230 - 1.250	Three-quarters charged
1.260 - 1.280	Fully charged

Don't measure specific gravity immediately after adding water. Ride the machine a few miles to ensure thorough mixing of the electrolyte.

It is most important to maintain batteries fully charged during cold weather. A fully charged battery freezes at a much lower temperature than does one which is partially discharged. Freezing temperature depends on specific gravity (see **Table 3**).

Table 3   BATTERY FREEZING TEMPERATURE

Specific Gravity	Freezing Temperature (Degrees F)
1.100	18
1.120	13
1.140	8
1.160	1
1.180	—6
1.200	—17
1.220	—31
1.240	—50
1.260	—75
1.280	—92

CHAPTER SIX

CARBURETORS

For proper operation, a gasoline engine must be supplied with fuel/air, mixed in proper proportions by weight. A mixture in which there is excess fuel is said to be rich. A lean mixture is one which contains insufficient fuel. It is the function of the carburetors to supply the proper mixture to the engine under all operating conditions.

CARBURETOR OPERATION

Major functional systems of a carburetor are a float and float valve mechanism for maintaining a constant fuel level in the float bowl; a pilot system for supplying fuel at low speeds; a main fuel system, which supplies the engine at medium and high speeds; and a starter system, which supplies the very rich mixture needed to start a cold engine. Operation of each system is discussed in the following paragraphs.

Float Mechanism

Figure 1 illustrates a typical float mechanism. Proper operation of the carburetor is dependent on maintaining a constant fuel level in the carburetor bowl. As fuel is drawn from the float bowl, the float level drops. When the float drops, the float valve moves away from its seat and allows fuel to flow past the valve and seat into the float bowl. As this occurs, the float is then raised, pressing the valve against its seat, thereby shutting off the flow of fuel. It can be seen from this discussion that a small piece of dirt can be trapped between the valve and seat, preventing the valve from closing and allowing fuel to rise beyond the normal level, resulting in flooding. **Figure 2** illustrates this condition.

Pilot System

Under idle or low speed conditions, at less than 1/8 throttle, the engine does not require much fuel or air, and the throttle valve is almost closed. A separate pilot system is required for operation under such conditions. **Figure 3** illustrates the operation of the pilot system. Air is drawn through the pilot air inlet and controlled by the pilot air screw. The air is then mixed with fuel drawn through the pilot jet. The air/fuel mixture then travels from the pilot outlet into the main air passage, where it is further mixed with air prior to being drawn into the engine. The pilot air screw controls idle mixture.

If proper idle and low speed mixture cannot be obtained within the normal adjustment range of the idle mixture screw, refer to **Table 1** for possible causes.

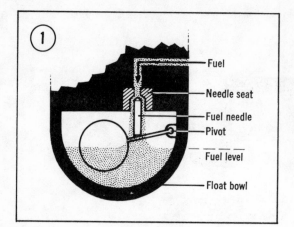

Fuel

Needle seat

Fuel needle

Pivot

Fuel level

Float bowl

Table 1	PILOT SYSTEM PROBLEMS
Too Rich	
Clogged pilot air intake	
Clogged air passage	
Clogged air bleed opening	
Pilot jet loose	
Too Lean	
Obstructed pilot jet	
Obstructed jet outlet	
Worn throttle valve	
Carburetor mounting loose	

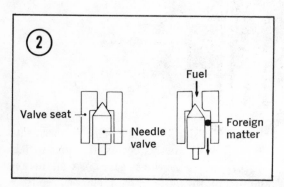

Valve seat

Needle valve

Fuel

Foreign matter

Main Fuel System

As the throttle is opened still more, up to about ¼ open, the pilot circuit begins to supply less of the mixture to the engine, as the main fuel system, illustrated in **Figure 4**, begins to function. The main jet, needle jet, jet needle, and air jet make up the main fuel circuit. As the throttle valve opens more than about ⅛ of its travel, air is drawn through the main port, and

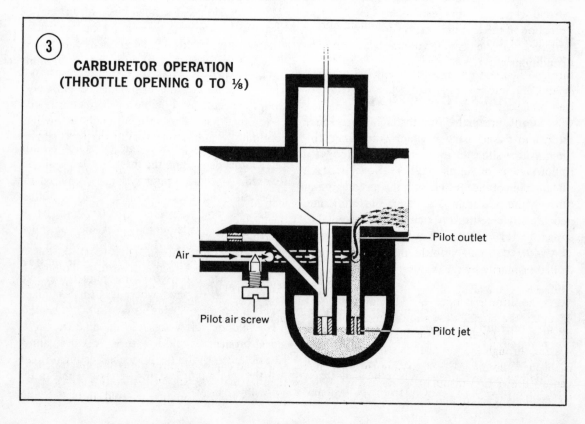

CARBURETOR OPERATION
(THROTTLE OPENING 0 TO ⅛)

Pilot outlet

Air

Pilot jet

Pilot air screw

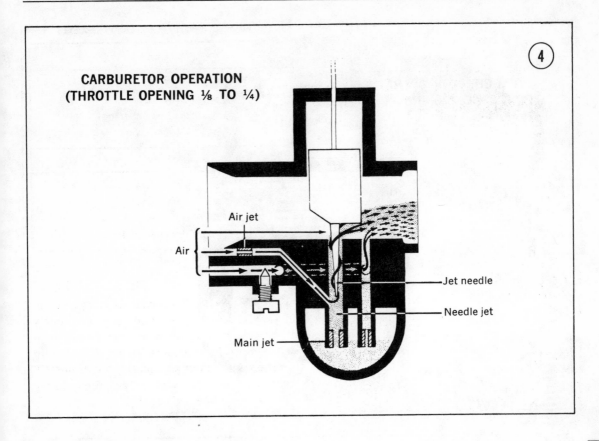

**CARBURETOR OPERATION
(THROTTLE OPENING ⅛ TO ¼)**

④

Air jet

Air

Jet needle

Needle jet

Main jet

passes under the throttle valve in the main bore. Velocity of the air stream results in reduced pressure around the jet needle. Fuel then passes through the main jet, past the needle jet and jet needle, and into the air stream where it is atomized and sent to the cylinder. As the throttle valve opens, more air flows through the carburetor, and the jet needle, which is attached to the throttle slide, rises to permit more fuel to flow.

A portion of the air bled past the air jet passes through the needle jet bleed air inlet into the needle jet, where the air is mixed with the main stream and atomized.

Airflow at small throttle openings is controlled primarily by the cutaway on the throttle slide.

As the throttle is opened wider, up to about ¾ open, the circuit draws air from 2 sources, as shown in **Figure 5**. The first source is air passing through the venturi; the second source is through the air jet. Air passing through the venturi draws fuel through the needle jet. The jet needle is tapered, and therefore allows more

fuel to pass. Air passing through the air jet passes to the needle jet to aid atomization of the fuel there.

Figure 6 illustrates the circuit at high speeds. The jet needle is withdrawn almost completely from the needle jet. Fuel flow is then controlled by the main jet. Air passing through the air jet continues to aid atomization of the fuel as described in the foregoing paragraphs.

Any dirt which collects in the main jet or in the needle jet obstructs fuel flow and causes a lean mixture. Any clogged air passage, such as the air bleed opening or air jet, may result in an overrich mixture. Other causes of a rich mixture are a worn needle jet, loose needle jet, or loose main jet. If the jet needle is worn, it should be replaced; however, it may be possible to effect a temporary repair by placing the needle jet clip in a higher groove.

Starter System

A cold engine requires a mixture much richer than normal. The starter system (**Figure 7**) supplies this fuel/air mixture for cold starts.

6

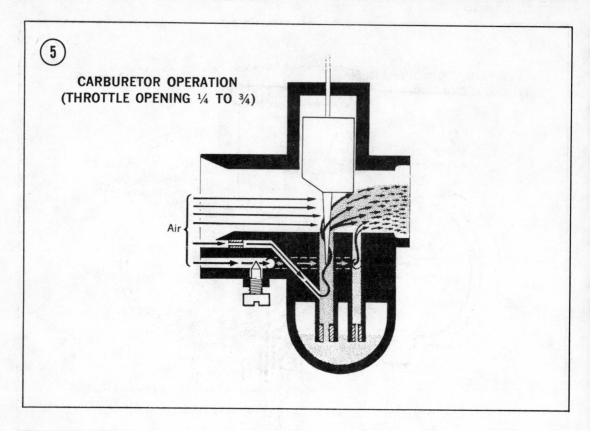

⑤

**CARBURETOR OPERATION
(THROTTLE OPENING ¼ TO ¾)**

Air

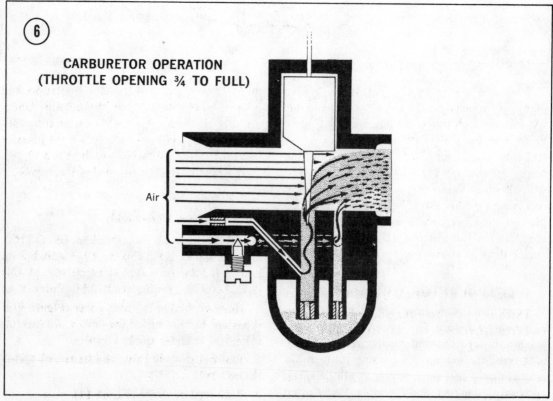

⑥

**CARBURETOR OPERATION
(THROTTLE OPENING ¾ TO FULL)**

Air

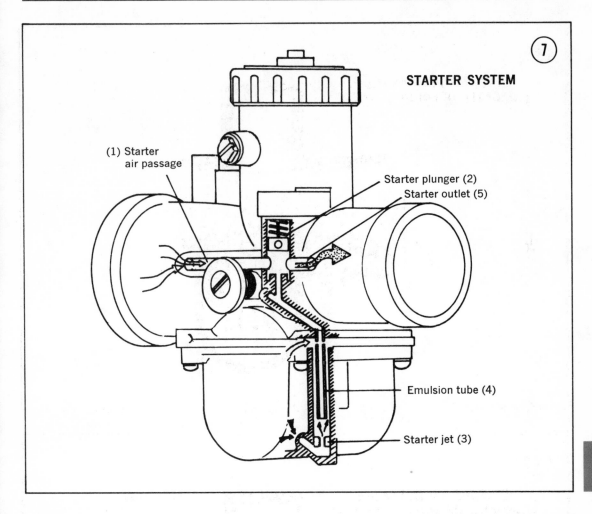

STARTER SYSTEM

(1) Starter air passage

Starter plunger (2)
Starter outlet (5)

Emulsion tube (4)

Starter jet (3)

6

When the starter lever is operated, starter plunger (2) opens. As the engine is cranked, air is drawn through starter air passage (1). Engine vacuum in the starter plunger chamber draws fuel from starter jet (3). Fuel passing from the starter jet through emulsion tube (4) is mixed with air which enters through a small hole. The fuel is then further mixed with air in the starter plunger chamber, where it is atomized. This atomized fuel/air mixture is then drawn into the engine through starter outlet (5).

CARBURETOR OVERHAUL

There is no set rule regarding frequency of carburetor overhaul. A carburetor used on a machine used primarily for street riding may go 5,000 miles without attention. If the machine is used under very dusty conditions, the carburetor might need an overhaul in less than 1,000

miles. Poor engine performance, hesitation, and little or no response to idle mixture adjustment are all symptoms of possible carburetor malfunction. As a general rule, it is good practice to overhaul the carburetors each time you perform a routine decarbonization of the engine.

VM Carburetor Disassembly

VM carburetors are installed on GT380, GT550, and early GT750 models. **Figure 8** is an exploded view of a typical carburetor of this type. Refer to it during disassembly and service.

1. Remove mixing chamber cover (**Figure 9**) if it has not been removed previously. Be careful; this cover is under spring pressure.

2. Pull out throttle valve and its return spring (**Figure 10**).

3. Remove float bowl (**Figure 11**).

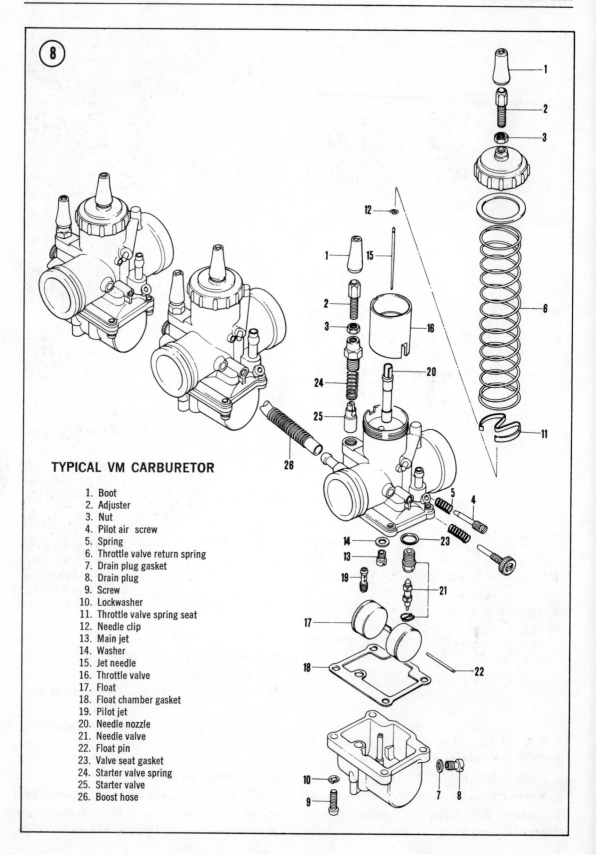

TYPICAL VM CARBURETOR

1. Boot
2. Adjuster
3. Nut
4. Pilot air screw
5. Spring
6. Throttle valve return spring
7. Drain plug gasket
8. Drain plug
9. Screw
10. Lockwasher
11. Throttle valve spring seat
12. Needle clip
13. Main jet
14. Washer
15. Jet needle
16. Throttle valve
17. Float
18. Float chamber gasket
19. Pilot jet
20. Needle nozzle
21. Needle valve
22. Float pin
23. Valve seat gasket
24. Starter valve spring
25. Starter valve
26. Boost hose

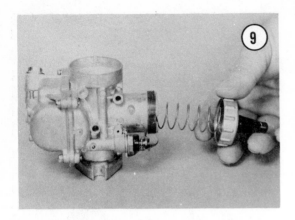

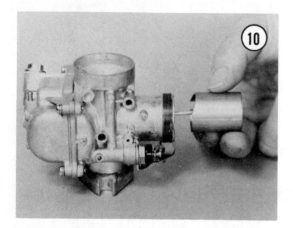

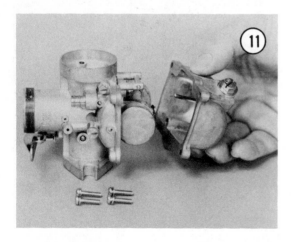

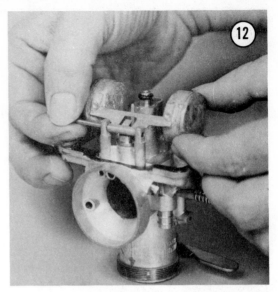

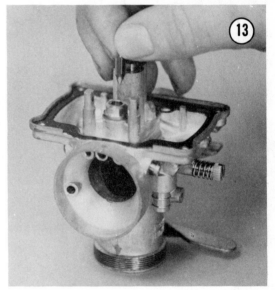

4. Pull out float pivot shaft (**Figure 12**), then gently remove float assembly.

5. Remove float needle (**Figure 13**).

6. Remove main jet and its washer (**Figure 14**).

7. Remove float valve seat and its washer (**Figure 15**).

8. Remove pilot jet (**Figure 16**).

9. Push out needle jet, using a plastic or fiber tool (**Figure 17**).

10. Remove idle speed and idle mixture screws. Take care not to lose their springs.

11. Reverse the disassembly procedure to assemble the carburetor.

BS Carburetor Disassembly

BS carburetors are installed on later GT750 models. Disassembly and service procedures are generally similar to those of VM carburetors.

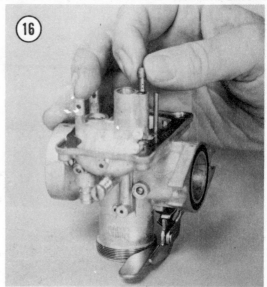

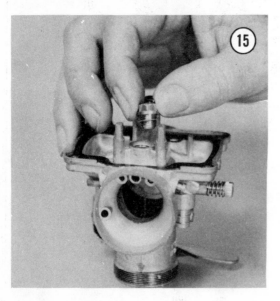

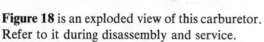

Figure 18 is an exploded view of this carburetor. Refer to it during disassembly and service.

Carburetor Inspection

Clean all parts in carburetor cleaning solvent. Dry them with compressed air. Clean jets and other delicate parts with compressed air after the float bowl has been removed. *Never* attempt to clean jets or passages by running a wire through them; to do so will cause damage and destroy their calibration. Do not use compressed air to clean an assembled carburetor, since the float and float valve can be damaged.

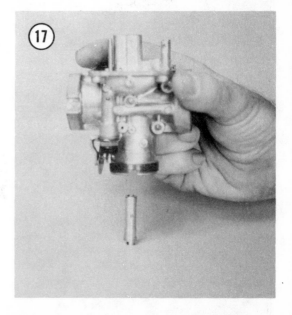

Shake the float to check for gasoline inside. If fuel leaks into the float, float chamber fuel level will rise, resulting in an overrich mixture. Replace the float if it is deformed or leaking.

Replace the float valve if its seating end is scratched or worn. Press the float valve gently with your finger and make sure that the valve seats properly. If the float valve does not seat properly, fuel will overflow, causing an overrich mixture and flooding the float chamber whenever the fuel petcock is open.

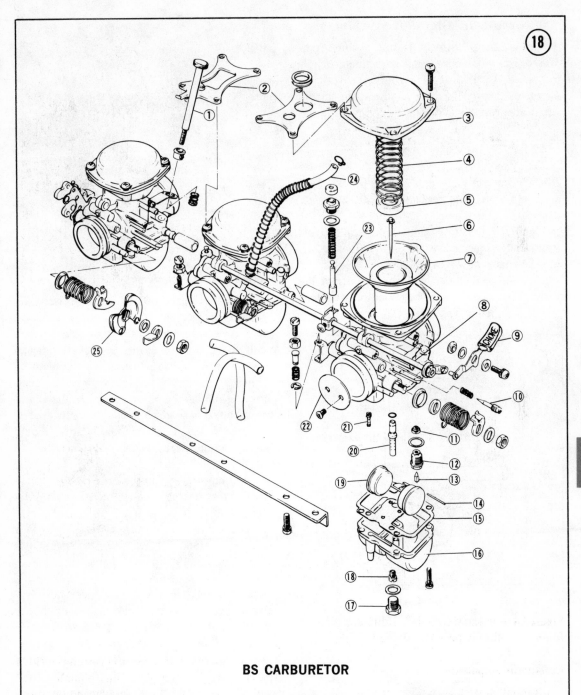

BS CARBURETOR

1. Throttle valve stop screw
2. Bracket
3. Mixing chamber top
4. Piston valve spring
5. Jet needle set plate
6. Jet needle
7. Piston valve
8. Starter rod
9. Choke lever

10. Pilot screw
11. Fuel strainer
12. Valve seat
13. Needle valve
14. Float arm pin
15. Float chamber gasket
16. Float chamber
17. Drain plug

18. Main jet
19. Float
20. Needle jet
21. Pilot jet
22. Throttle valve
23. Starter plunger
24. Fuel hose
25. Pulley

CARBURETOR ADJUSTMENT

Carburetor adjustment is not normally required except for occasional adjustment of idling speed, or at time of carburetor overhaul. Refer to Chapter Two for routine adjustments which are normally made during engine tune-up.

Float Level

The machine was delivered with the float level adjusted correctly. Rough riding, a bent float arm, or a worn float needle and seat can cause the float level to change.

Figure 19 illustrates float level adjustment. Remove the carburetor, then the float bowl. Measure distance (D) between the gasket surface and the top of the float, with the carburetor inverted. Distance (D) must be equal for each float and as specified in **Table 2**.

A. Bend tang to adjust float level

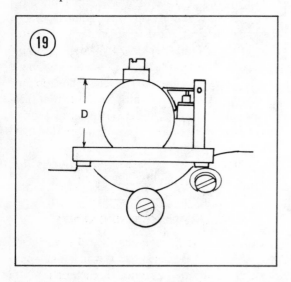

Table 2   FLOAT LEVEL

Carburetor Model	Distance D	
	Inches	(Millimeters)
VM24SC	1.01	(25.7)
VM28SC	1.01	(25.7)
VM32SC	1.06	(27.0)
BS40	1.09	(27.6)

If float level is not correct, bend tang on the float (A, **Figure 20**) as required.

Speed Range Adjustments

The carburetors on your machine were designed to provide the proper mixture under all operating conditions. Little or no benefit will result from experimenting. However, unusual operating conditions such as sustained operation at high altitudes or unusually high or low temperatures may make modifications to the standard specifications desirable. The adjustments described in the following paragraphs should only be undertaken if the rider has definite reason to believe they are required. Make the tests and adjustments in the order specified.

Make a road test at full throttle for final determination of main jet size. To make such a test, operate the motorcycle at full throttle for at least 2 minutes, then shut the engine off, release the clutch, and bring the machine to a stop.

If at full throttle, the engine runs "heavily," the main jet is too large. If the engine runs better by closing the throttle slightly, the main jet is too small. The engine will run at full throttle evenly and regularly if the main jets are of correct size.

After each such test, remove and examine the spark plugs. The insulators should have a light tan color. If the insulator has black sooty deposits, the mixture is too rich. If there are signs of intense heat, such as a blistered white appearance, the mixture is too lean.

As a general rule, main jet size should be reduced approximately 5 percent for each 3,000 feet (1,000 meters) above sea level.

Refer to **Table 3**. Note that the center carburetor main jet is different from that in each of the left and right cylinders on models GT550 and GT750.

Table 3   MAIN JETS

Model	Standard Main Jet
VM24SC	80
VM28SC (center)	97.5
VM28SC (left and right)	95
VM32SC (center)	100
VM32SC (left and right)	102.5
BS40 (center)	107.5
BS40 (left and right)	110

Table 4 lists symptoms caused by rich and lean mixtures.

Table 4   MIXTURE TROUBLESHOOTING

Condition	Symptom
Rich mixture	Rough idle
	Black exhaust smoke
	Hard starting, especially when hot
	"Blubbering" under acceleration
	Black deposits in exhaust pipe
	Gas-fouled spark plug
	Poor gas mileage
	Engine performs worse as it warms up
Lean mixture	Backfiring
	Rough idle
	Overheating
	Hesitation upon acceleration
	Engine speed varies at fixed throttle
	Loss of power
	White color on spark plug insulator
	Poor acceleration

Adjust the pilot air screws as follows.

1. Turn in each pilot air screw until it seats lightly, then back it out about 1½ turns, except for BS40 carburetors. Back out idle mixture screws on these carburetors ¾ turn.

2. Start the engine and warm it to normal operating temperature.

3. Turn in each idle speed screw equally until the engine runs slower and begins to falter.

4. Adjust each pilot air screw as required to make the engine run smoothly.

5. Repeat Steps 3 and 4 to achieve the lowest stable idle speed.

Next, determine proper throttle valve cutaway size. With the engine running at idle, open the throttle. If the engine does not accelerate smoothly from idle, turn each pilot air screw in (clockwise) slightly to richen the mixture. If the condition still exists, return each air screw to its original position and replace each throttle valve with one which has a smaller cutaway. If engine operation is worsened by turning the air screw, replace each throttle valve with one which has a larger cutaway. All carburetors should have a throttle valve with the same size cutaway.

For operation at ¼-¾ throttle opening, adjustment is made with the jet needle. Operate the engine at ½ throttle in a manner similar to that for the full throttle test described earlier. To richen the mixture, place the jet needle clip in a lower groove. Conversely, placing the clip in a higher groove leans the mixture. Note that the center carburetor on model GT750 uses a different needle jet than do the carburetors for the left and right cylinders.

A summary of carburetor adjustments is given in **Table 5**.

CARBURETOR COMPONENTS

The following paragraphs describe various components of the carburetor which may be changed to vary performance characteristics.

Throttle Valve

The throttle valve cutaway controls airflow at small throttle openings. Cutaway sizes are numbered. Larger numbers permit more air to flow at a given throttle opening and result in a leaner mixture. Conversely, smaller numbers result in a richer mixture.

Jet Needle

The jet needle, together with the needle jet, controls mixture at medium speeds. As the throttle valve rises to increase airflow through

6

Table 5   CARBURETOR ADJUSTMENT SUMMARY

Throttle opening	Adjustment	If too rich	If too lean
0 - ⅛	Air screw	Turn out	Turn in
⅛ - ¼	Throttle valve cutaway	Use larger cutaway	Use smaller cutaway
¼ - ¾	Jet needle	Raise clip	Lower clip
¾ - full	Main jet	Use smaller number	Use larger number

the carburetor, the jet needle rises with it. The tapered portion of the jet needle rises from the needle jet and allows more fuel to flow, thereby providing the engine with the proper mixture at up to about ¾ throttle opening. Grooves at the top of the jet needle permit adjustment of mixture ratio in the medium speed range.

Needle Jet

The needle jet operates with the jet needle. Several holes are drilled through the side of the needle jet. These holes meter airflow from the air jet. Air from the air jet is bled into the needle jet to assist in atomization of fuel.

Main Jet

The main jet controls the mixture at full throttle, and has some effect at lesser throttle openings. Each main jet is stamped with a number. Fuel flow is approximately proportional to the number. Larger numbers provide a richer mixture.

**MISCELLANEOUS
CARBURETOR PROBLEMS**

Water in the carburetor float bowl and sticking carburetor slide valves can result from careless washing of the motorcycle. To remedy the problem, remove and clean the carburetor bowl, main jet, and any other affected parts. Be sure to cover the air intake when washing the machine.

Be sure that the ring nut on the top of the carburetor is secure. Also be sure that carburetor mounting bolts are tight.

If gasoline leaks past the float bowl gasket, high speed fuel starvation may occur. Varnish deposits on the outside of the float bowl are evidence of this condition.

Dirt in the fuel may lodge in the float valve and cause an overrich mixture. As a temporary measure, tap the carburetor lightly with any convenient tool to dislodge the dirt. Clean the fuel tank, petcock, fuel line, and carburetor at the first opportunity, should this situation occur.

CHAPTER SEVEN

FRAME, SUSPENSION, AND STEERING

FRAME

Frames on these machines are of welded steel tubing (**Figure 1**). Service on the frame is limited to inspection for bending of the frame members or cracked welds. Examine the frame carefully in the event that the machine has been subjected to a collision or hard spill.

HANDLEBAR

The handlebar is made from solid drawn steel tubing. Most of the manual controls (**Figure 2**) are mounted on the handlebar assembly. Wiring from the switches on the handlebar assembly is routed to the headlight assembly, where it is connected to the main wiring harness.

Disassembly

Handlebar removal is generally similar for all models. The following steps are set forth as a guide:

1. Pull the clutch cable, then disconnect it from the clutch lever.

2. Loosen the adjustment nut at the front brake, then remove the cable at the front brake hand lever.

3. Remove the mixing chamber caps from each carburetor, then remove the throttle cables from the throttle valves.

4. Disconnect the wiring from the handlebar inside the headlamp housing.

5. Remove the clamp bolts, then lift off the handlebar.

Inspection

Check the throttle cable for smooth operation and for stretching of the inner cable. Be sure that all controls operate smoothly. Lubricate the throttle cables, also the throttle grip. If the machine was spilled, check for bending of the handlebar.

Reassembly

Reverse disassembly procedure to assemble handlebar. Observe the following notes:

1. Be sure that no wires are pinched between the handlebar and switch bodies.

2. Adjust throttle grip tension as desired with the throttle grip adjuster. Be sure to tighten the locknut after adjustment.

3. Be sure to install new cotter pins in the handlebar lever bolts.

FRONT FORKS

Figure 3 is an exploded view of a typical front fork assembly. Service procedures are generally similar for all models.

7

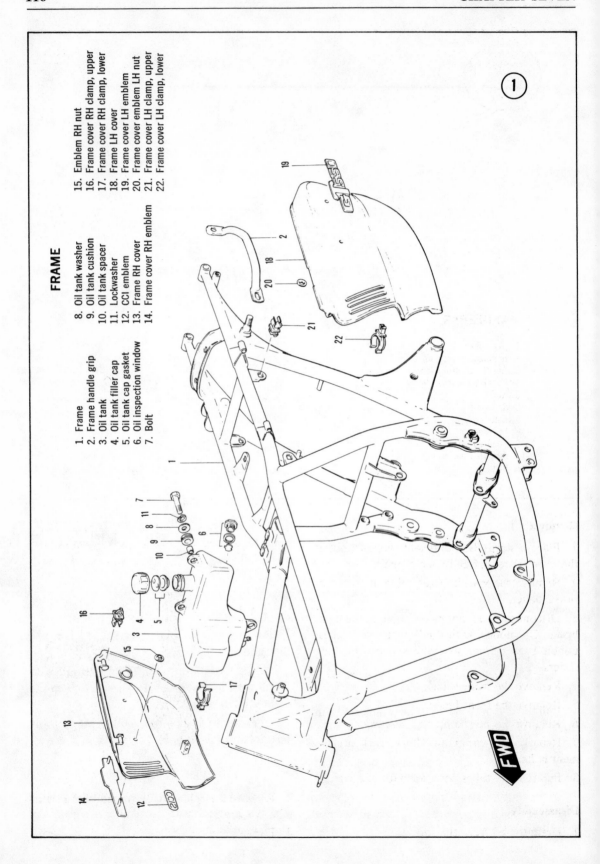

FRAME

1. Frame
2. Frame handle grip
3. Oil tank
4. Oil tank filler cap
5. Oil tank cap gasket
6. Oil inspection window
7. Bolt
8. Oil tank washer
9. Oil tank cushion
10. Oil tank spacer
11. Lockwasher
12. CCI emblem
13. Frame RH cover
14. Frame cover RH emblem
15. Emblem RH nut
16. Frame cover RH clamp, upper
17. Frame cover RH clamp, lower
18. Frame LH cover
19. Frame cover LH emblem
20. Frame cover emblem LH nut
21. Frame cover LH clamp, upper
22. Frame cover LH clamp, lower

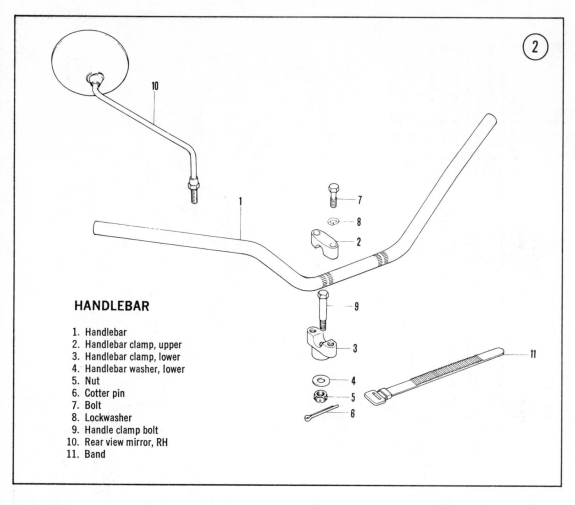

HANDLEBAR

1. Handlebar
2. Handlebar clamp, upper
3. Handlebar clamp, lower
4. Handlebar washer, lower
5. Nut
6. Cotter pin
7. Bolt
8. Lockwasher
9. Handle clamp bolt
10. Rear view mirror, RH
11. Band

Removal

1. Place a sturdy box under the engine so that the front wheel is free of the ground.

2. Remove the speedometer cable at the front brake panel.

3. Disconnect the front brake cable at the front brake. On models with dual front disc brakes, unbolt both caliper assemblies from the fork sliders.

4. Remove the front wheel.

5. Remove the front fender.

6. Remove the headlamp and housing.

7. Remove the upper and lower fork attachment bolts.

8. Pull the fork tubes downward for removal.

Disassembly

1. Drain the oil from the fork.

2. Remove the snap ring at the top of the outer tube (**Figure 4**). The whole assembly may then be pulled apart.

3. Remove the bolt at the lower end of the outer tube (**Figure 5**).

4. Remove the oil seal.

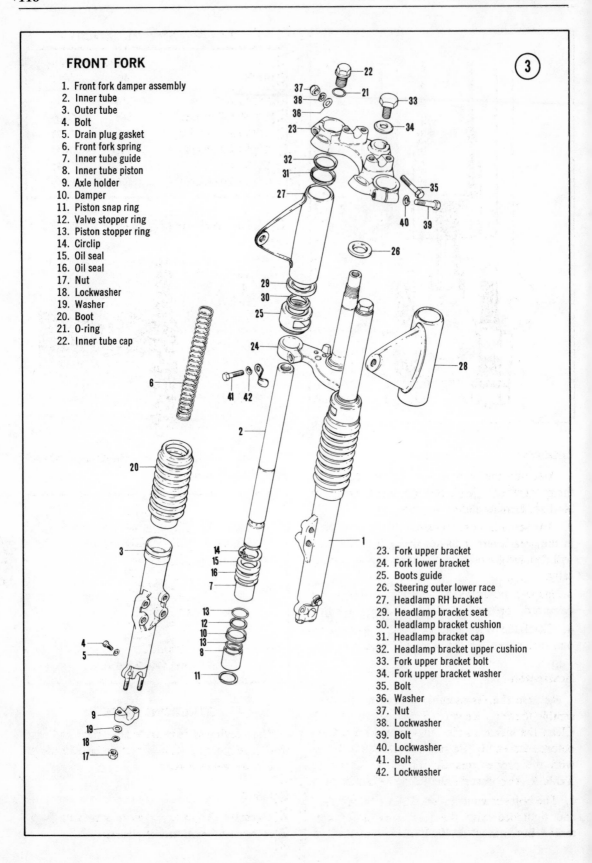

FRONT FORK

1. Front fork damper assembly
2. Inner tube
3. Outer tube
4. Bolt
5. Drain plug gasket
6. Front fork spring
7. Inner tube guide
8. Inner tube piston
9. Axle holder
10. Damper
11. Piston snap ring
12. Valve stopper ring
13. Piston stopper ring
14. Circlip
15. Oil seal
16. Oil seal
17. Nut
18. Lockwasher
19. Washer
20. Boot
21. O-ring
22. Inner tube cap

23. Fork upper bracket
24. Fork lower bracket
25. Boots guide
26. Steering outer lower race
27. Headlamp RH bracket
29. Headlamp bracket seat
30. Headlamp bracket cushion
31. Headlamp bracket cap
32. Headlamp bracket upper cushion
33. Fork upper bracket bolt
34. Fork upper bracket washer
35. Bolt
36. Washer
37. Nut
38. Lockwasher
39. Bolt
40. Lockwasher
41. Bolt
42. Lockwasher

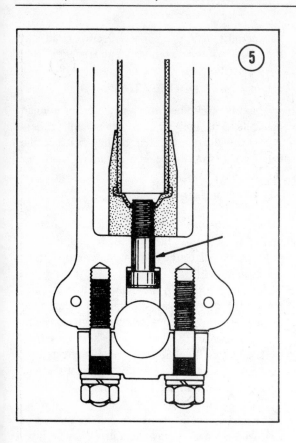

Inspection

1. Assemble the inner and outer tubes, then slide them together. Check for looseness, noise, or binding. Replace defective parts.

2. Any scratches or roughness on the inner tube in the area where it passes through the oil seal will damáge the oil seal. Examine this area carefully.

3. Inspect the dust seal carefully. If this seal is damaged, foreign material will enter the fork.

4. Check the fork spring for wear. If you replace one spring, replace the other one also.

Reassembly

Reverse the disassembly procedure to reassemble the fork. Be sure to replace the oil seal. Clean the inside of the outer tube with solvent before reassembly. Be sure to refill the fork legs with the proper quantity of oil as shown in **Table 1**. Also observe the following notes.

1. The bolt shown in Figure 5 must be installed and tightened with the fork completely bottomed, but without the fork spring installed.

Table 1   FORK OIL CAPACITY

Model	Front Fork (each leg)	
	cc	(oz.)
GT380 J, K	210	(7.1)
GT380 (all others)	145	(4.9)
GT550 J, K, L	235	(7.9)
GT550 (all others)	160	(5.4)
GT750 J, K	235	(7.9)
GT750 (all others)	160	(5.4)

2. Use a seal driver (**Figure 6**) to install the oil seal.

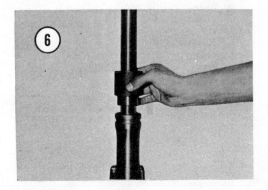

3. Install each fork spring with its tapered end downward (**Figure 7**).

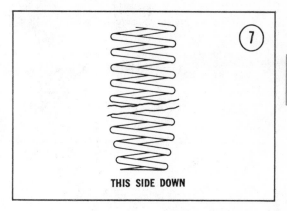

THIS SIDE DOWN

STEERING STEM

The steering stem is made from steel and cast iron. The steering stem pivots on ball bearings within the steering head.

Removal

1. Remove the steering stem attaching bolt, then the two fork attaching bolts.

2. Remove the steering stem lock nut and lockwasher.

3. Loosen the steering stem nut slightly, then raise and support the steering stem.

4. Remove the steering stem nut by hand.

5. Pull the steering stem downward to remove it from the steering head. Be careful that you don't drop and damage any of the steel balls.

6. Remove the inner races by tapping them out with a long punch and hammer.

7. Use a hammer and chisel to remove the lower outer race.

Inspection

1. Check the balls and races for wear, cracks, or rust. Replace the entire bearing assembly if any part is damaged. Do not use any combination of new and used parts.

2. Check the steering stem for bending or cracked welds.

Installation

1. Tap the inner bearing races into position with a bearing installation tool.

2. Pack the lower inner race with grease, then install the steel balls. The grease will hold the balls in position.

3. Pack the upper inner race with grease, then install the steel balls.

4. Insert the steering stem into the steering head.

5. Install the steering stem nut, lockwasher, and lock nut.

6. Tighten the lock nut, then turn the steering stem nut counterclockwise until there is no play between the steering stem and steering head, but the front fork turns smoothly and freely.

DRIVE CHAIN

The drive chain becomes worn after prolonged use. Wear in the pins, bushings, and rollers causes the chain to stretch. Sliding between the roller surface and sprocket teeth also contributes to wear.

Inspection

Inspect the drive chain periodically. Pay particular attention to cracks in the rollers and link plates, and replace the chain if there is any doubt about its condition.

Adjust free play in the chain so that there is about 0.6-0.8 in. (15-20mm) vertical play (**Figure 8**) in the center of the chain run with the machine on the ground. Be sure to adjust each side equally. The rear brake is affected by any chain adjustment. Be sure to adjust the rear brake after you adjust the chain.

If the chain has become so worn that it must be replaced, use a chain breaker to remove it (**Figure 9**). Suzuki bikes are equipped with flare-type chain joints (**Figure 10**) for additional chain strength.

Clean the chain, then lubricate it at intervals not exceeding 1,000 miles (1,500 km), or more often if necessary.

WHEELS AND TIRES

Various sizes of wheels and tires are installed on Suzuki motorcycles. Consult the specifications to determine the size of your machine.

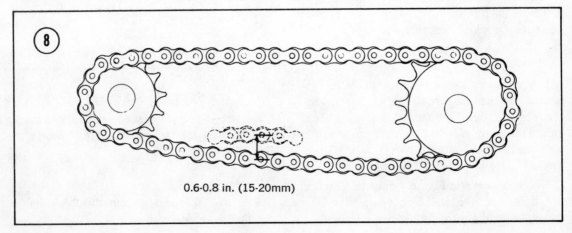

0.6-0.8 in. (15-20mm)

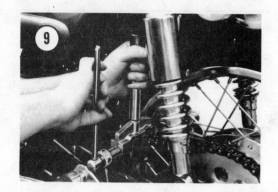

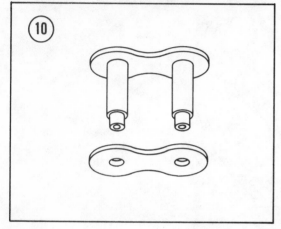

Rims

The rim supports the tire and provides rigidity to the wheel assembly. A rim band protects the inner tube from abrasion.

Spokes

The spokes support the weight of the motorcycle and rider, and transmit tractive and braking forces.

Check the spokes periodically for looseness or bending. A bent or otherwise faulty spoke will adversely affect neighboring spokes, and should therefore be replaced immediately. To remove the spoke, completely unscrew the threaded portion, then remove the bent end from the hub.

Spokes tend to loosen as the machine is used. Retighten each spoke one turn, beginning with those on one side of the hub, then those on the other side. Tighten the spokes on a new machine after the first 50 miles of operation, then at 50-mile intervals until they no longer loosen.

If the machine is subjected to particularly severe service, check the spokes frequently.

Wheel Balance

An unbalanced wheel results in unsafe riding conditions. Depending on the degree of unbalance and the speed of the motorcycle, the rider may experience anything from a mild vibration to a violent shimmy which may even result in loss of control. Apply balance weights (**Figure 11**) to the spokes on the light side of the wheel to correct this condition.

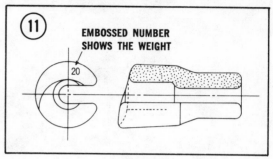

EMBOSSED NUMBER SHOWS THE WEIGHT

Before you attempt to balance the wheel, check to be sure that the wheel bearings are in good condition and properly lubricated, and that the brakes do not drag, so that the wheel rotates freely. With the wheel free of the ground, spin it slowly and allow it to come to rest by itself. Add balance weights to the spokes on the light side as required, so that the wheel comes to rest at a different position each time it is spun. Balance weights are available in measures of 10, 20, and 30 grams. Remove the drive chain when you balance the rear wheel.

Front Hub

Figure 12 is an exploded view of a typical front wheel and hub assembly. The entire hub assembly rotates on two ball bearings. The speedometer gears transmit front wheel rotation to the speedometer.

If the bearings are worn, tap them out with a small hammer and long punch, then replace them. Examine the lips of the oil seals for wear or damage, then replace them if necessary. Examine the brake drum for grooves or scratches.

Rear Hub

Figures 13 and 14 are exploded views of typical rear wheels and hubs. Service on the rear hub is similar to that on the front hub, with the

7

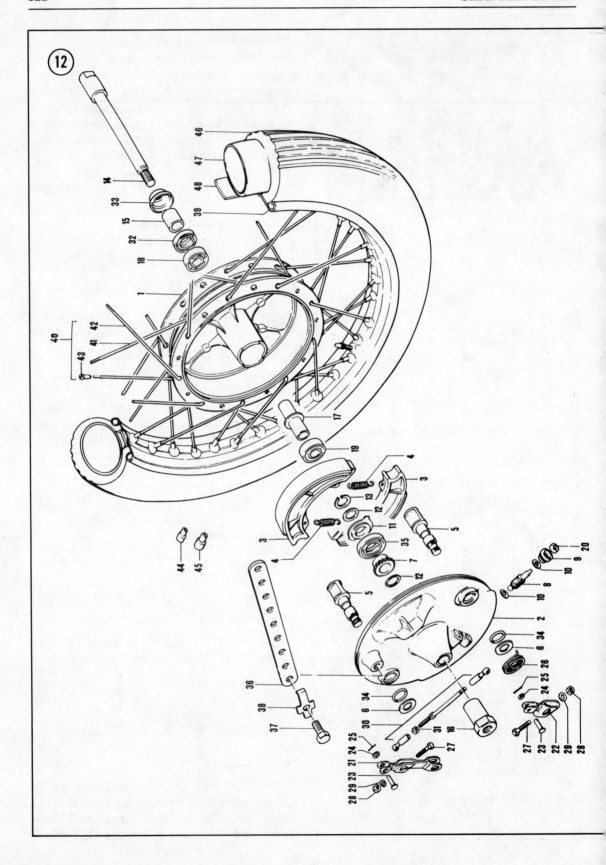

FRONT WHEEL

1. Front wheel hub
2. Front brake anchor panel
3. Front brake shoe
4. Brake shoe spring
5. Front brake cam
6. Front brake cam washer
7. Speedometer gear
8. Speedometer pinion
9. Speedometer pinion bushing
10. Speedometer gear thrust washer
11. Speedometer gear driver
12. Speedometer thrust washer
13. Circlip
14. Front axle
15. Front axle spacer
16. Front axle nut
17. Front hub bearing spacer
18. Bearing
19. Bearing
20. Speedometer pinion oil seal
21. Front brake cam lever (1)
22. Front brake cam lever (2)
23. Cam lever pivot pin
24. Washer
25. Cotter pin
26. Cam lever return spring
27. Front brake cam lever bolt
28. Nut
29. Washer
30. Brake cam lever rod set
31. Nut
32. Front hub oil seal
33. Front hub dust seal cover
34. Front brake cam O-ring
35. Anchor panel oil seal
36. Front torque link
37. Front torque link bolt
38. Front torque link washer
39. Wheel rim
40. Front spoke set
41. Wheel spoke, inner
42. Wheel spoke, outer
43. Spoke nipple
44. Wheel balance weight (1)
45. Wheel balance weight (2)
46. Front tire
47. Wheel inner tube
48. Wheel inner tube protector

addition of checking and replacing the shock absorber if it is worn or damaged.

Checking Wheel Runout

To measure runout of the wheel rim, support the wheel so that it is free to rotate. Position a dial indicator as shown in **Figure 15**. Observe the dial indicator as you rotate the wheel through a complete revolution. Runout limit for all models is 0.07 in. (2.0mm). Excessive runout may be caused by a bent rim or loose spokes. Repair or replace as required.

If runout is excessive, mount the wheel on an adjusting stand, and adjust each spoke as required, using a spoke wrench.

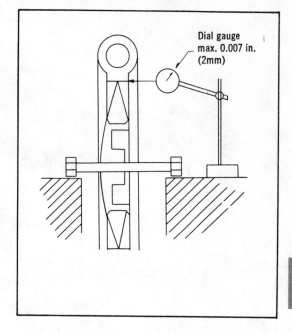

Dial gauge
max. 0.007 in.
(2mm)

Wheel Alignment

Check wheel alignment as shown in **Figure 16**. If wheels are misaligned more than 0.12 in. (3mm), correct with both drive chain adjusters as required. If alignment can't be corrected by adjustment, check the frame, front fork, swinging arm, and wheel rims for bending.

Wheel Bearings

Wheel bearings should be serviced at 4,000-mile (6,000-km) intervals. After removal, clean them thoroughly in solvent, then check them for smooth operation. If they are OK, repack

7

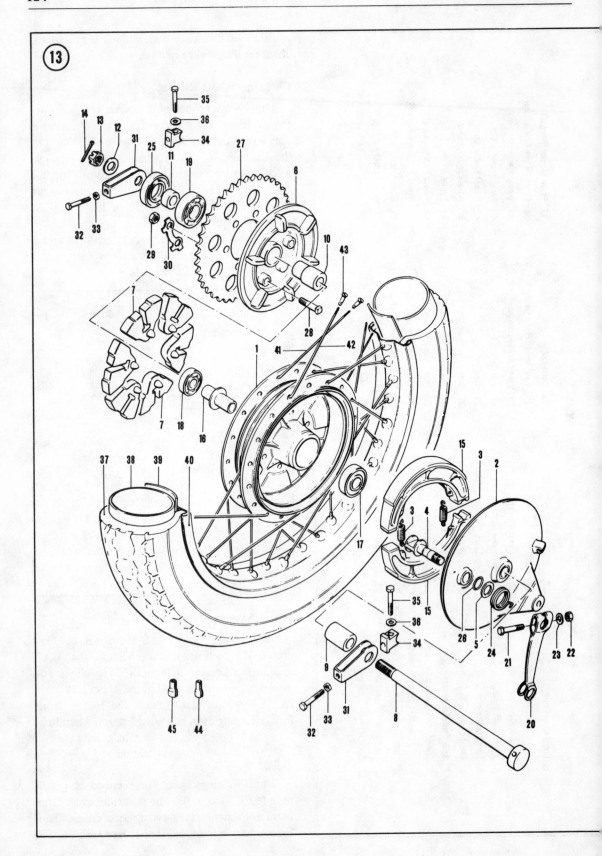

REAR WHEEL

1. Rear wheel hub
2. Rear brake anchor panel
3. Brake shoe spring
4. Rear brake cam
5. Rear brake cam washer
6. Rear sprocket drum
7. Rear hub shock absorber
8. Rear axle
9. Rear axle RH spacer
10. Sprocket drum retainer
11. Rear axle spacer, LH
12. Rear axle nut washer
13. Rear axle nut
14. Cotter pin
15. Rear brake shoe
16. Rear hub bearing spacer
17. Rear hub bearing, RH
18. Rear hub bearing, LH
19. Rear sprocket drum bearing
20. Rear brake cam lever
21. Bolt
22. Nut
23. Washer
24. Cam lever return spring
25. Sprocket drum oil seal
26. Rear brake cam O-ring
27. Rear sprocket
28. Rear sprocket bolt
29. Nut
30. Rear sprocket lockwasher
31. Chain adjuster
32. Chain adjuster bolt
33. Nut
34. Chain adjuster support
35. Bolt
36. Washer
37. Rear tire
38. Wheel inner tube
39. Inner tube protector
40. Wheel rim
41. Wheel spoke, inner
42. Wheel spoke, outer
43. Wheel spoke nipple
44. Wheel balance weight (1)
45. Balance weight

with fresh grease. Be sure that wheel grease seals are in good condition.

INTERNAL EXPANDING BRAKES

Earlier models are equipped with internal expanding brakes on both wheels.

Front wheels are equipped with dual leading shoe front brakes. Two camshafts, one for each shoe, are used in this design. As each camshaft turns, its forces its associated shoe into contact with the brake drum. As the drum turns, its movement tends to increase pressure on the brake shoe against the brake drum, thereby increasing braking power.

Later models with front disc brakes have internal expanding brakes on rear wheels only.

Disassembly

Pull the brake shoes, with its springs attached, from the brake panel. Remove the springs with pliers, if necessary, after the shoes are removed. Install the shoes with the springs attached.

Inspection

Examine the brake lining for oil or other foreign material. Dirt imbedded in the brake lining may be removed with a wire brush. Replace both brake shoes if the lining is worn excessively. Measure brake lining wear as shown in **Figure 17**. Replace both brake shoes if either is worn to less than wear limit given in **Table 2**.

Measure inner diameter of each brake drum. Replace any drum worn beyond the wear limit. See **Table 3**.

If the brake shoe return springs are worn or stretched, the brake shoes will not retract fully and the brakes may drag. Replace the springs if they are stretched.

The brake camshaft O-ring prevents water or dust from corroding the camshaft. Be sure that the dust seal is in good condition and is properly installed.

Replace the camshaft if it is worn or badly corroded. To remove the camshaft, tap it out with a soft mallet. Remove any light corrosion with emery paper. Lubricate the camshaft with

7

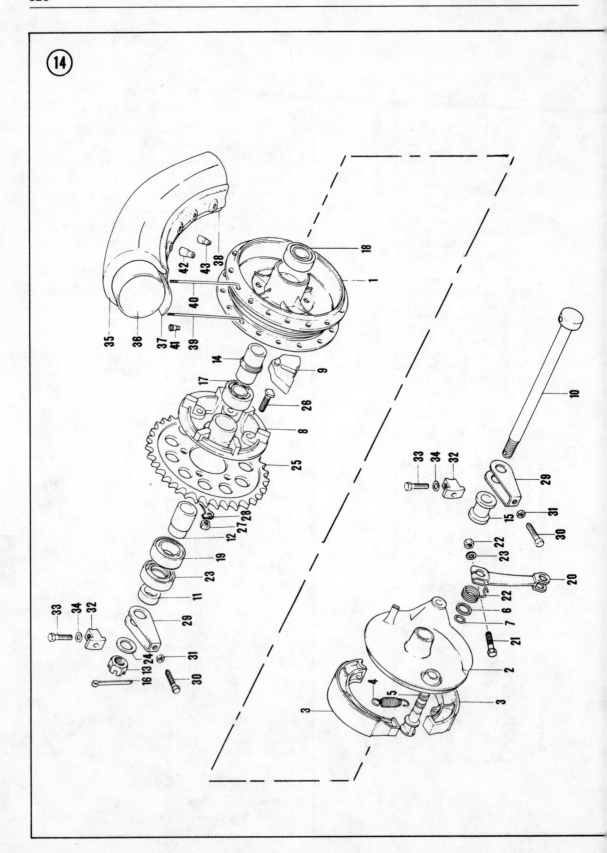

REAR WHEEL

1. Rear wheel hub
2. Rear wheel panel
3. Rear brake shoe
4. Rear brake shoe spring
5. Rear brake cam
6. Washer
7. O-ring
8. Rear sprocket drum
9. Rear hub shock absorber
10. Rear axle
11. Rear axle spacer, RH
12. Rear hub bearing retainer
13. Nut
14. Hub bearing spacer
15. Rear axle spacer, LH
16. Cotter pin
17. Wheel hub bearing, RH
18. Wheel hub bearing, LH
19. Sprocket drum bearing
20. Rear brake cam lever
21. Bolt
22. Brake cam lever return spring
23. Sprocket drum oil seal
24. Rear axle nut washer
25. Rear sprocket
26. Rear sprocket bolt
27. Nut
28. Rear sprocket washer
29. Chain adjuster
30. Bolt
31. Nut
32. Chain adjuster support
33. Bolt
34. Washer
35. Tire
36. Tube
37. Inner tube protector
38. Wheel rim
39. Inner spoke
40. Outer spoke
41. Spoke nipple
42. No. 2 balancer
43. No. 1 balancer

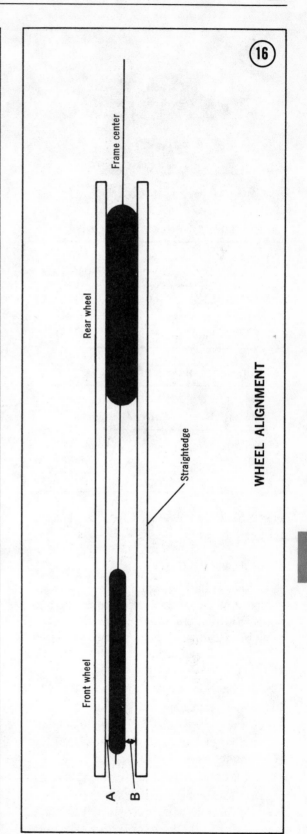

WHEEL ALIGNMENT

7

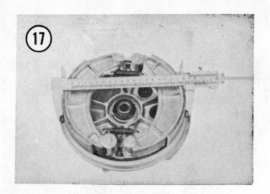

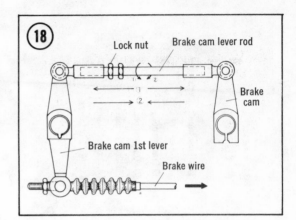

Table 2   BRAKE SHOE LIMITS

| Model | Wear Limit | |
	Inches	(Millimeters)
GT380	6.93	(176)
GT550	7.64	(194)
GT750	7.64	(194)

Table 3   BRAKE DRUM DIAMETER

| Model | Wear Limit | |
	Inches	(Millimeters)
GT380	7.11	(180.7)
GT550	7.90	(200.7)
GT750	7.90	(200.7)

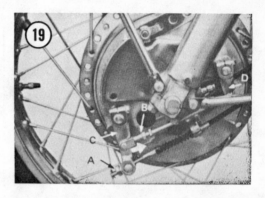

perpendicular to the brake lever when the front brake is fully applied (**Figure 20**).

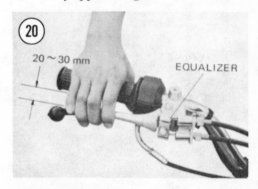

grease before installation. Check the camshaft for free rotation.

Front Brake Adjustment

Do not adjust the brake lever connector (**Figure 18**) except after replacement of brake shoes or if front brake performance has become poor as a result of only one shoe contacting the brake drum. To adjust the connector lever, proceed as follows.

1. See **Figure 19**. Loosen cable adjuster (A).

2. Loosen connecting rod locknut (B).

3. Lightly press lever (C), and while holding it in position, turn the connecting rod until lever (D) does not move.

4. Tighten connecting rod locknut (B).

5. Turn each cable adjuster at the front brake lever to provide about one inch (20-30mm) free-play at the brake lever, with the equalizer

Rear Brake Adjustment

Adjust the rear brake by turning the adjustment nut on the rear brake lever. There should be 0.8-1.2 in. (20-30mm) free-play at the brake pedal (**Figure 21**) before braking action occurs.

DISC BRAKES

Later models are equipped with disc brakes on front wheels. Model GT750 has dual discs

and calipers for greater stopping power. Service procedures for all models are similar; differences are pointed out where they exist. **Figure 22** shows location of major disc brake components.

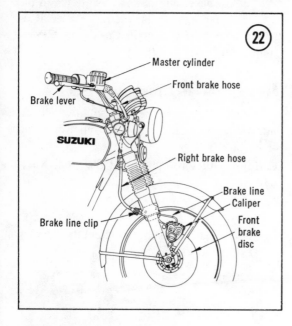

Master cylinder
Front brake hose
Brake lever
SUZUKI
Right brake hose
Brake line
Caliper
Brake line clip
Front brake disc

Brake Fluid

To check brake fluid level, the motorcycle must be upright and level. It is suggested that it be placed on its center stand, with the front wheel pointed straight ahead.

Refer to **Figure 23**. Remove cover (A) and diaphragm (B). If brake fluid level is below mark (C), replenish with brake fluid meeting specification DOT 3 or DOT 4. Brake fluid meeting those specifications will be so marked on its container.

WARNING
Do not use any other type fluid in this system.

Brake fluid is hydroscopic, that is, it absorbs moisture from the atmosphere, so certain precautions must be taken in its use and handling.

1. Never use brake fluid from old or unsealed containers.

2. Do not replenish the reservoir when there is a possibility of rain entering it.

3. Change brake fluid yearly, or immediately if there is reason to believe it may be contaminated with water. See *Changing Brake Fluid.*

CAUTION
Brake fluid will damage paint and instrument lenses. To avoid spurting brake fluid, do not operate brake lever when reservoir cover is removed.

Bleeding Brakes

Air entrapped in the brake system causes serious loss of braking power. Symptoms of this condition are a soft, spongy feel, and increased travel of the brake hand lever. When this situation occurs, it is necessary to bleed the system. Note that this operation is much easier to perform if an assistant is available.

1. Locate the bleeder screw, then remove its dust cover (**Figure 24**). On Model GT750, perform this operation on the left caliper first.

2. Slip one end of a length of plastic tubing over the bleeder screw. Submerge the other end in a vessel containing brake fluid (**Figure 25**).

NOTE: *The end of the tubing must remain submerged during the entire bleeding procedure.*

7

3. Be sure reservoir is full. It must be at least ½ full during this entire procedure. Replace its cover.

4. Pressurize the system by operating the hand lever several times, then holding it tightly in brake-applied position.

5. Open bleeder valve ½ turn, then press brake lever to its fully applied position. Tighten the bleeder screw. Do not release brake lever until bleeder screw is tightened.

6. Repeat Steps 4 and 5 until no more air bubbles are expelled, and hand lever action is firm.

> NOTE: *Check brake fluid level periodically during this procedure. Reservoir must remain at least ½ full.*

7. Remove bleeder hose and replace dust cover. Replenish reservoir.

8. On model GT750, repeat Steps 1 through 7 for the right-hand caliper assembly.

9. Do not reuse brake fluid drained from the system.

Changing Brake Fluid

Moisture tends to accumulate in brake fluid, thereby lowering its boiling point and causing a loss of braking power. It is therefore recommended that fluid be replaced at least once a year, or more often if necessary.

To change brake fluid, open bleeder screw, then operate the brake hand lever until no more brake fluid runs out. Refill the reservoir, then bleed the system as described in the foregoing section.

Brake Pad Inspection

Inspect brake pads periodically. Replace them as a set whenever any pad is worn down to the red line marked on its circumference. Pads should also be replaced in the event of contamination by oil or grease.

Pad Replacement (GT380 and GT550)

Before replacing brake pads, remove all dirt and foreign material from the front wheel and brake caliper.

1. Support motorcycle so that the front wheel is free.

2. Remove front wheel and brake disc as an assembly.

3. Remove pad No. 2 by taking out its retaining screw (**Figure 26**).

4. Operate brake lever several times to force out pad No. 2.

5. Refer to **Figure 27**. Apply a very light coat of brake pad grease (supplied in pad replacement kit) to the circumference and back surface of pad No. 1. Do not apply any other type of grease, and do not allow any grease to get on

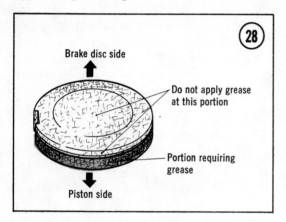

the pad's friction surface (**Figure 28**). Do not apply any grease to pad No. 2.

6. Press pad No. 1 into caliper holder.

7. Install pad No. 2, then replace its retaining screw. Be sure that pad No. 2 is not cocked when it is installed.

8. Install front wheel.

9. Operate brake lever several times.

10. Bleed brake system if necessary.

Pad Replacement (GT750)

Before replacing brake pads, remove all dirt and foreign material from the front wheel and brake caliper assemblies.

1. Refer to **Figure 29**. Remove cover (1) and guide (2).

2. Loosen both left caliper retaining bolts (3), as shown in **Figure 30**. Do not disconnect the brake line.

3. Remove left caliper assembly, then support it with string or wire.

4. Remove front wheel and both brake discs as an assembly.

5. Replace left caliper assembly.

6. Insert a spacer, approximately ¼ in. (6mm) thick between both pads of the right caliper assembly. Hold this spacer in position with a rubber band.

7. Replace both pads in the left caliper. Follow Steps 3 through 7 of foregoing *Pad Replacement (GT380 and GT550)*.

8. Remove spacer from caliper and install it between pads of left caliper.

9. Replace pads in right caliper, following same procedure.

10. Remove spacer from left caliper.

11. Remove left caliper assembly and support it out of the way. Do not disconnect brake line.

12. Install front wheel.

13. Install left caliper assembly.

14. Replace cover and guide.

15. Operate brake hand lever several times.

16. Bleed brake system if necessary.

Master Cylinder Removal

Figure 31 is an exploded view of the master cylinder on models GT380 and GT550. Master

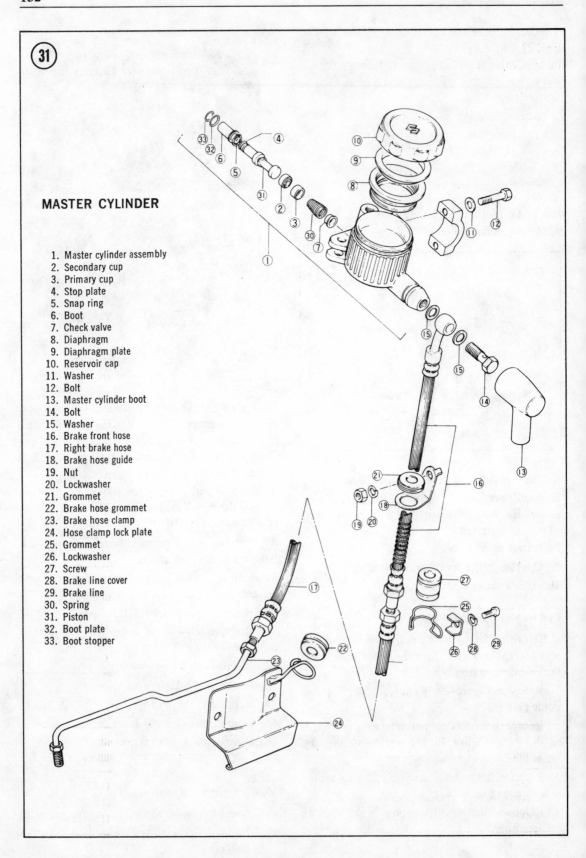

MASTER CYLINDER

1. Master cylinder assembly
2. Secondary cup
3. Primary cup
4. Stop plate
5. Snap ring
6. Boot
7. Check valve
8. Diaphragm
9. Diaphragm plate
10. Reservoir cap
11. Washer
12. Bolt
13. Master cylinder boot
14. Bolt
15. Washer
16. Brake front hose
17. Right brake hose
18. Brake hose guide
19. Nut
20. Lockwasher
21. Grommet
22. Brake hose grommet
23. Brake hose clamp
24. Hose clamp lock plate
25. Grommet
26. Lockwasher
27. Screw
28. Brake line cover
29. Brake line
30. Spring
31. Piston
32. Boot plate
33. Boot stopper

cylinders on GT750 models are similar (**Figure 32**), but differ slightly in details. Refer to the applicable illustration during service. Numbers in parentheses refer to the legends in these illustrations.

1. Remove stoplight switch.

2. Place a rag under union bolt (14) to catch any brake fluid, then remove union bolt to disconnect brake hose from master cylinder.

3. Drain brake fluid from reservoir.

Master Cylinder Disassembly

1. Remove brake lever.

2. Remove boot stopper, then boot. Take care not to damage boot.

3. Remove snap ring (5).

4. Remove piston, primary cup, spring, and check valve.

> NOTE: *It is recommended that a new master cylinder kit be installed whenever master cylinder is disassembled.*

5. Clean all parts in fresh brake fluid only.

> **WARNING**
> *Never use any petroleum solvents on brake system components exposed to brake fluid.*

Master Cylinder Inspection

1. Measure master cylinder inner diameter. Replace it if its inner diameter exceeds the wear limit specified in **Table 4**.

2. Measure piston diameter as shown in **Figure 33**. Replace it if it is worn to its wear limit. See **Table 5**.

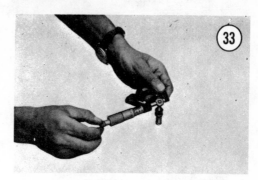

Master Cylinder Reassembly

Reverse the disassembly procedure to reassemble the master cylinder. Be sure that all parts are installed correctly. **Figure 34** illustrates proper assembly order and orientation. Bleed the system after installation.

When installing master cylinder, be sure that there is about 0.08 in. (2mm) gap between it and the switch housing (**Figure 35**). Note also that it should be installed so that its cover is horizontal with the bike in normal riding position.

Table 4   MASTER CYLINDER INNER DIAMETER

Model	Standard Diameter		Wear Limit	
	Inch	(Millimeters)	Inch	(Millimeters)
GT380	0.5512 - 0.5527	(14.00 - 14.04)	0.5531	(14.05)
GT550	0.5512 - 0.5227	(14.00 - 14.04)	0.5531	(14.05)
GT750	0.6248 - 0.6264	(15.87 - 15.91)	0.6268	(15.92)

Table 5   MASTER CYLINDER PISTON DIAMETER

Model	Standard Diameter		Wear Limit	
	Inch	(Millimeters)	Inch	(Millimeters)
GT380	0.5496 - 0.5504	(13.96 - 13.98)	0.5488	(13.94)
GT550	0.5496 - 0.5504	(13.96 - 13.98)	0.5488	(13.94)
GT750	0.6232 - 0.6240	(15.83 - 15.85)	0.6224	(15.81)

7

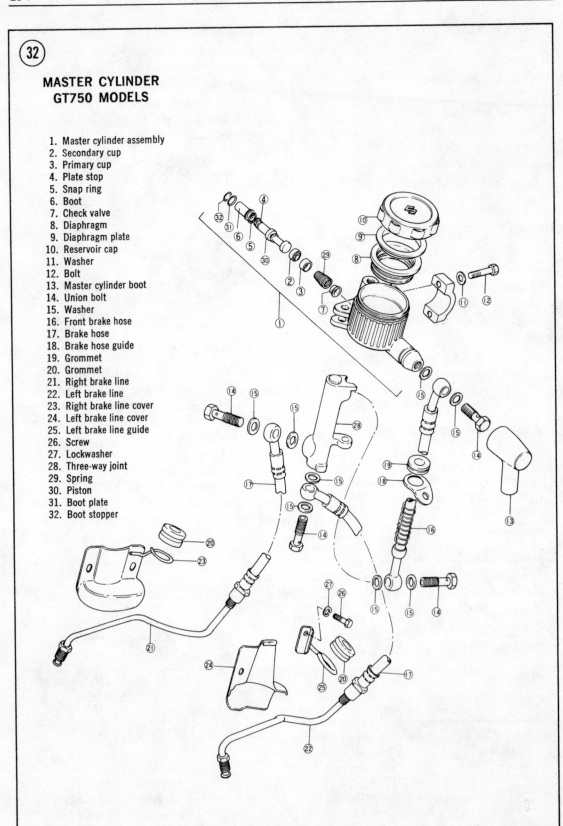

32

MASTER CYLINDER
GT750 MODELS

1. Master cylinder assembly
2. Secondary cup
3. Primary cup
4. Plate stop
5. Snap ring
6. Boot
7. Check valve
8. Diaphragm
9. Diaphragm plate
10. Reservoir cap
11. Washer
12. Bolt
13. Master cylinder boot
14. Union bolt
15. Washer
16. Front brake hose
17. Brake hose
18. Brake hose guide
19. Grommet
20. Grommet
21. Right brake line
22. Left brake line
23. Right brake line cover
24. Left brake line cover
25. Left brake line guide
26. Screw
27. Lockwasher
28. Three-way joint
29. Spring
30. Piston
31. Boot plate
32. Boot stopper

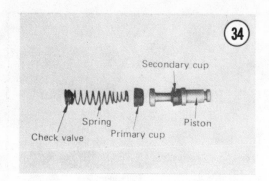

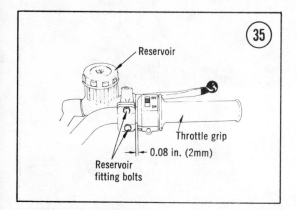

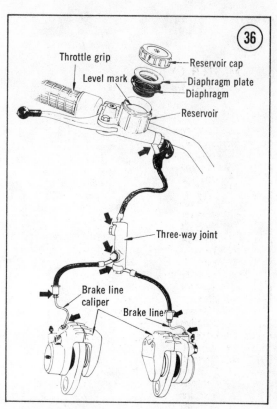

Brake Hoses and Tubing

Periodically check hoses, tubing, and connections for wear, swelling, corrosion, leaks, or any other type of deterioration. **Figure 36** illustrates locations to check.

Caliper Removal and Disassembly

Figure 37 is an exploded view of a typical caliper assembly. Refer to it during service.

1. Remove brake line.
2. Remove retaining bolts.
3. Remove caliper assembly.
4. Remove both shaft bolts (**Figure 38**).

5. Separate inner and outer caliper bodies.
6. Remove caliper holder.
7. Remove O-rings from caliper shafts.
8. Remove caliper shafts.
9. Remove piston boot.
10. Refer to **Figure 39**. Force out piston by blowing compressed air into caliper assembly. Catch piston as it comes out.
11. Remove piston seal (**Figure 40**).

7

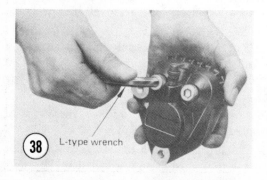

NOTE: *It is recommended that a caliper overhaul kit be installed whenever caliper is disassembled.*

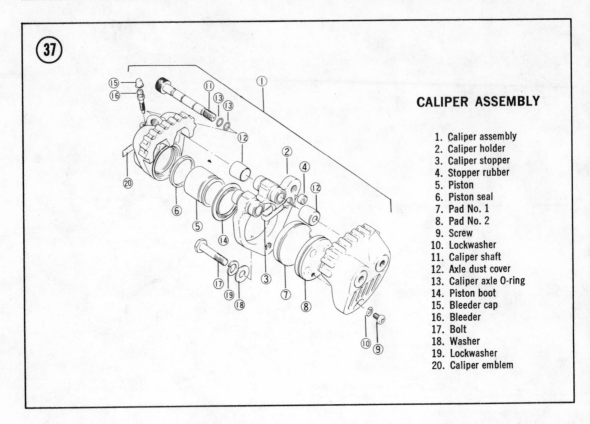

(37)

CALIPER ASSEMBLY

1. Caliper assembly
2. Caliper holder
3. Caliper stopper
4. Stopper rubber
5. Piston
6. Piston seal
7. Pad No. 1
8. Pad No. 2
9. Screw
10. Lockwasher
11. Caliper shaft
12. Axle dust cover
13. Caliper axle O-ring
14. Piston boot
15. Bleeder cap
16. Bleeder
17. Bolt
18. Washer
19. Lockwasher
20. Caliper emblem

(40)

Piston seal

(41)

Caliper Inspection

1. Measure inner bore of caliper. Replace if it is worn to more than 1.5047 in. (38.22mm). Standard bore is 1.5031 to 1.5039 in. (38.18 to 38.20mm).

2. Measure piston outer diameter (**Figure 41**). Replace if it is worn to less than 1.5000 in. (38.10mm). Standard piston diameter is 1.5020-1.5031 in. (38.15-38.18mm).

3. If piston seals must be reused, be sure they are in good condition.

4. Check piston boot for damage.

5. Be sure that pads are not worn to their limit lines.

Caliper Reassembly

Caliper reassembly and installation is generally the reverse of removal. Observe the following notes.

1. Refer to **Figure 42**. Apply caliper shaft grease (available at Suzuki dealers) to both shafts in the area shown. Do not substitute another type of grease.

2. Lubricate piston and its bore liberally with brake fluid before assembly.

3. Be sure that piston seal (**Figure 43**) is not cocked or twisted when it is installed.

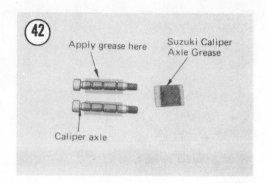

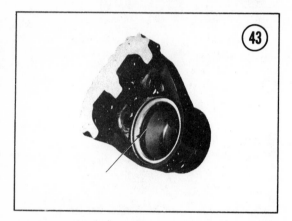

4. Refer to the applicable section for installation of brake pads.

5. Bleed system after assembly.

6. Ride the bike, then check that front wheel does not drag.

NOTE: *It is recommended that a caliper overhaul kit be installed at intervals not exceeding 2 years.*

Brake Disc

Brake discs are made of stainless steel and should have a long service life. Note that brake disc runout or wear can, however, adversely affect brake performance.

1. Refer to **Figure 44**. Set up a dial indicator so that runout may be measured. Standard runout tolerance is 0.004 in. (0.1mm). If runout exceeds 0.012 in. (0.3mm), the cause may be either the front wheel bearing or the disc itself. Replace whichever is defective.

2. Measure brake disc thickness (**Figure 45**). Standard thickness is 0.276 in. (7.00mm). Re-

place the disc if it is worn to 0.236 in. (6.00mm) or less at any point.

3. Be sure that no oil or grease gets onto the brake disc.

4. If the brake disc is removed, torque its retaining bolts to 11-18 ft.-lb. (1.5-2.5 mkg). Be sure that lockwasher tabs are secure.

SHOCK ABSORBERS

Figure 46 is a sectional view of a typical rear shock absorber. The major parts of the shock absorber are a spring, and hydraulic damping mechanism encased within the inner and outer shells. The shock absorbers may be adjusted to suit various riding conditions. Adjust both sides equally.

To remove the shock absorbers, remove the mounting bolts. Do not damage the rubber bushings as you remove and replace the bolts.

Check the damping force by attempting to compress and extend the units quickly. If there is not marked difference between the effort required to operate the unit quickly, or slowly, or if there are any oil leaks, replace the shock absorber.

7

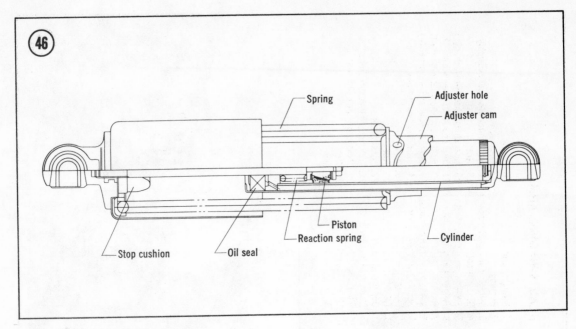

Spring · Adjuster hole · Adjuster cam · Piston · Reaction spring · Cylinder · Stop cushion · Oil seal

SWINGING ARM

Figure 47 illustrates a typical swinging arm assembly. The entire assembly pivots up and down on the pivot shaft. The rear part of the swinging arm is attached to the motorcycle frame through the shock absorbers.

Disassembly

1. Remove the drive chain.
2. Remove the rear sprocket.
3. Remove the pivot shaft.
4. Remove the swinging arm.

Inspection

The pivot section is susceptible to wear, especially in the bushings and shaft. Examine these parts carefully. Replace the pivoit shaft if it is bent more than 0.02 in. (0.5mm). Replace the bushings and/or the shaft if clearance between shaft and bushings exceeds 0.014 in. (0.35mm). Shimmy, wander, and wheel hop are common symptoms of worn swinging arm bushings. If either of the arms is bent, the rear wheel will be cut of alignment. Examine the weld carefully. Replace the entire swinging arm assembly if the weld is cracked.

Reassembly

1. Grease the pivot shaft liberally.
2. Apply thread lock cement to the pivot shaft threads before you install the nut.

AIR CLEANER

The air cleaner filters abrasive particles from air on its way to the engine. If the air cleaner becomes clogged, power drops and fuel consumption increases. Remove dirt from the air cleaner by brushing or blowing with an air hose.

Never operate the bike without an air cleaner. Since fuel and air passes through the crankcase, dirt drawn in may damage crankshaft and connecting rod bearings in only a few miles.

EXHAUST PIPES
AND MUFFLERS

Carbon deposits within the exhaust pipe and muffler cause the engine to lose power. Remove the baffle tubes and clean carbon from them by heating with a torch, then tapping the baffle tube lightly with any convenient tool. Clean carbon from the curved exhaust pipes by scraping with a screwdriver or by running a used chain through the pipe.

Be sure that the rubber connectors are not hardened or cracked. Replace them if they are no longer serviceable.

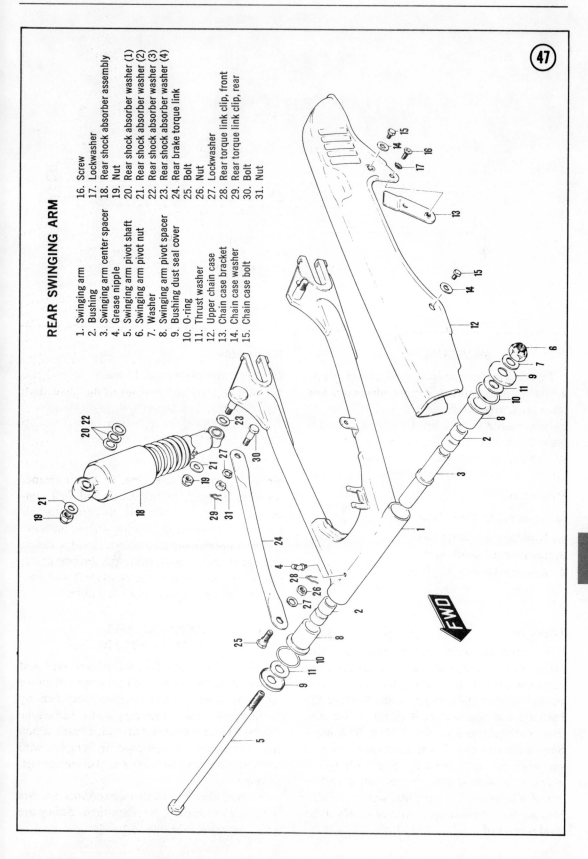

REAR SWINGING ARM

1. Swinging arm
2. Bushing
3. Swinging arm center spacer
4. Grease nipple
5. Swinging arm pivot shaft
6. Swinging arm pivot nut
7. Washer
8. Swinging arm pivot spacer
9. Bushing dust seal cover
10. O-ring
11. Thrust washer
12. Upper chain case
13. Chain case bracket
14. Chain case washer
15. Chain case bolt
16. Screw
17. Lockwasher
18. Rear shock absorber assembly
19. Nut
20. Rear shock absorber washer (1)
21. Rear shock absorber washer (2)
22. Rear shock absorber washer (3)
23. Rear shock absorber washer (4)
24. Rear brake torque link
25. Bolt
26. Nut
27. Lockwasher
28. Rear torque link clip, front
29. Rear torque link clip, rear
30. Bolt
31. Nut

7

CHAPTER EIGHT

TROUBLESHOOTING

Diagnosing motorcycle ills is relatively simple if you use orderly procedures and keep a few basic principles in mind.

Never assume anything. Don't overlook the obvious. If you are riding along and the bike suddenly quits, check the easiest, most accessible problem spots first. Is there gasoline in the tank? Is the gas petcock in the "on" or "reserve" position? Has a spark plug wire fallen off? Check the ignition switch. Sometimes the weight of keys on a key ring may turn the ignition off suddenly.

If nothing obvious turns up in a cursory check, look a little further. Learning to recognize and describe symptoms will make repairs easier for you or a mechanic at the shop. Describe problems accurately and fully. Saying that "it won't run" isn't the same as saying "it quit on the highway at high speed and wouldn't start," or that "it sat in my garage for three months and then wouldn't start."

Gather as many symptoms together as possible to aid in diagnosis. Note whether the engine lost power gradually or all at once, what color smoke (if any) came from the exhausts and so on. Remember that the more complex a machine is, the easier it is to troubleshoot because symptoms point to specific problems.

You don't need fancy equipment or complicated test gear to determine whether repairs can be attempted at home. A few simple checks could save a large repair bill and time lost while the bike sits in a dealer's service department. On the other hand, be realistic and don't attempt repairs beyond your abilities. Service departments tend to charge heavily for putting together a disassembled engine that may have been abused. Some won't even take on such a job— so use common sense; don't get in over your head.

OPERATING REQUIREMENTS

An engine needs three basics to run properly: correct gas/air mixture, compression, and a spark at the right time. If one or more are missing, the engine won't run. The electrical system is the weakest link of the three. More problems result from electrical breakdowns than from any other source. Keep that in mind before you begin tampering with carburetor adjustments and the like.

If a bike has been sitting for any length of time and refuses to start, check the battery for a charged condition first, and then look to the gasoline delivery system. This includes the tank, fuel petcocks, lines, and the carburetors. Rust may have formed in the tank, obstructing fuel flow. Gasoline deposits may have gummed up carburetor jets and air passages. Gasoline tends to lose its potency after standing for long periods. Condensation may contaminate it with water. Drain old gas and try starting with a fresh tankful.

Compression or the lack of it, usually enters the picture only in the case of older machines. Worn or broken pistons, rings, and cylinder bores could prevent starting. Generally a gradual power loss and harder and harder starting will be readily apparent in this case.

STARTING DIFFICULTIES

Check gas flow first. Remove the gas cap and look into the tank. If gas is present, pull off a fuel line at the carburetor and see if gas flows freely. If none comes out the fuel tap may be shut off, blocked by rust or foreign matter, or the fuel line may be stopped up or kinked. If the carburetor is getting usable fuel, turn to the electrical system next.

Check that the battery is charged by turning on the lights or by beeping the horn. Refer to your owner's manual for starting procedures with a dead battery. Have the battery recharged if necessary.

Pull off a spark plug cap, remove the spark plug, and reconnect the cap. Lay the plug against the cylinder head so its base makes a good connection, and turn the engine over with the kick-starter. A fat, blue spark should jump across the electrodes. If there is no spark, or only a weak one, there is electrical system trouble. Check for a defective plug by replacing it with a known good one. Don't assume a plug is good just because it's new.

Once the plug has been cleared of guilt, but there's still no spark, start backtracking through the system. If the contact at the end of the spark plug wire can be exposed, it can be held about ⅛ inch from the head while the engine is turned over to check for a spark. Remember to hold the wire only by its insulation to avoid a nasty shock. If the plug wires are dirty, greasy, or wet, wrap a rag around them so you don't get shocked. If you do feel a shock or see sparks along the wire, clean or replace the wire and/or its connections.

If there's no spark at the plug wire, look for loose connections at the coil and battery. If all seems in order there, check next for oily or dirty contact points. Clean points with electrical contact cleaner, or a strip of paper. On battery ignition models, with the ignition switch turned on, open and close the points manually with a screwdriver.

No spark at the points with this test indicates a failure in the ignition system. Refer to Chapter Five (*Electrical System*) for detailed troubleshooting procedures for the entire system and its individual components. Refer to Chapter Two (*Periodic Maintenance*) for checking and setting ignition timing.

Note that spark plugs of the incorrect heat range (too cold) may cause hard starting. Set gaps to specifications. If you have just ridden through a puddle or washed the bike and it won't start, dry off plugs and plug wires. Water may have entered the carburetor and fouled the fuel under these conditions, but wet plugs and wires are the more likely problem.

If a healthy spark occurs at the right time, and there is adequate gas flow to the carburetor, check the carburetor itself at this time. Make sure all jets and air passages are clean, check float level, and adjust if necessary. Shake the float to check for gasoline inside it, and replace or repair as indicated. Check that the carburetors are mounted snugly, and no air is leaking past the mountings. Check for a clogged air filter.

Compression may be checked in the field by turning the kickstarter by hand and noting that an adequate resistance is felt, or by removing a spark plug and placing a finger over the plug hole and feeling for pressure.

An accurate compression check gives a good idea of the condition of the basic working parts of the engine. To perform this test, you need a compression gauge. The motor should be warm.

1. Remove the plug on the cylinder to be tested and clean out any dirt or grease.

2. Insert the tip of the gauge into the hole, making sure it is seated correctly.

3. Open the throttle all the way and make sure the chokes on the carburetors are open.

4. Crank the engine several times and record the highest pressure indication on the gauge. Perform this test on each cylinder. Refer to

8

Chapter Two (*Periodic Maintenance*) to interpret results.

POOR IDLING

Poor idling may be caused by incorrect carburetor adjustment, incorrect timing, or ignition system defects. Check the gas cap vent for an obstruction.

MISFIRING

Misfiring can be caused by a weak spark or dirty plugs. Check for fuel contamination. Run the machine at night or in a darkened garage to check for spark leaks along the plug wires and under the spark plug cap. If misfiring occurs only at certain throttle settings, refer to the carburetor chapter for the specific carburetor circuits involved. Misfiring under heavy load, as when climbing hills or accelerating, is usually caused by bad spark plugs.

FLAT SPOTS

If the engine seems to die momentarily when the throttle is opened and then recovers, check for a dirty main jet in the carburetor, water in the fuel, or an excessively lean mixture.

POWER LOSS

Poor condition of rings, pistons, or cylinders will cause a lack of power and speed. Ignition timing should be checked.

OVERHEATING

If the engine seems to run too hot all the time, be sure you are not idling it for long periods. Air-cooled engines are not designed to operate at a standstill for any length of time. Heavy stop and go traffic is hard on a motorcycle engine. Spark plugs of the wrong heat range can burn pistons. An excessively lean gas mixture may cause overheating. Check ignition timing. Don't ride in too high a gear. Broken or worn rings may permit compression gases to leak past them, heating heads and cylinders excessively. Check oil level and use the proper grade lubricants.

Water-cooled engines require an adequate supply of coolant and sufficient airflow through the radiator. Coolant will boil away if the radiator pressure cap is not in good condition, or if a sufficient concentration of antifreeze is not maintained.

BACKFIRING

Check that the timing is not advanced too far. Check fuel for contamination.

ENGINE NOISES

Experience is needed to diagnose accurately in this area. Noises are hard to differentiate and harder yet to describe. Deep knocking noises usually mean main bearing failure. A slapping noise generally comes from loose pistons. A light knocking noise during acceleration may be a bad connecting rod bearing. Pinging, which sounds like marbles being shaken in a tin can, is caused by ignition advanced too far or gasoline with too low an octane rating. Pinging should be corrected immediately or damage to pistons will result. Compression leaks at the head-cylinder joint will sound like a rapid on and off squeal.

PISTON SEIZURE

Piston seizure is caused by incorrect piston clearances when fitted, fitting rings with improper end gap, too thin an oil being used, incorrect spark plug heat range, or incorrect ignition timing. Overheating from any cause may result in seizure.

EXCESSIVE VIBRATION

Excessive vibration may be caused by loose motor mounts, worn engine or transmission bearings, loose wheels, worn swinging arm bushings, a generally poor running engine, broken or cracked frame, or one that has been damaged in a collision. See also *Poor Handling*.

CLUTCH SLIP OR DRAG

Clutch slip may be due to worn plates, improper adjustment, or glazed plates. A dragging clutch could result from damaged or bent plates, improper adjustment, or uneven clutch spring pressure.

POOR HANDLING

Poor handling may be caused by improper tire pressures, a damaged frame or swinging arm, worn shocks or front forks, weak fork springs, a bent or broken steering stem, misaligned wheels, loose or missing spokes, worn tires, bent handlebars, worn wheel bearing, or dragging brakes.

BRAKE PROBLEMS

Sticking brakes may be caused by broken or weak return springs, improper cable or rod adjustment, or dry pivot and cam bushings. Grabbing brakes may be caused by greasy linings which must be replaced. Brake grab may also be due to out-of-round drums or linings which have broken loose from the brake shoes. Glazed linings or glazed brake pads will cause loss of stopping power.

LIGHTING PROBLEMS

Bulbs which continuously burn out may be caused by excessive vibration, loose connections that permit sudden current surges, poor battery connections, or installation of the wrong type bulb.

A dead battery or one which discharges quickly may be caused by a faulty generator or rectifier. Check for loose or corroded terminals. Shorted battery cells or broken terminals will keep a battery from charging. Low water level will decrease a battery's capacity. A battery left uncharged after installation will sulphate, rendering it useless.

A majority of light and horn or other electrical accessory problems are caused by loose or corroded ground connections. Check those first, and then substitute known good units for easier troubleshooting.

TROUBLESHOOTING GUIDE

The following quick reference guide (**Table 1**) summarizes part of the troubleshooting process. Use it to outline possible problem areas, then refer to the specific chapter or section involved.

Table 1   TROUBLESHOOTING GUIDE

Item	Problem or Cause	Things to Check
Hard starting	Defective ignition system	Spark plug condition Breaker point condition Ignition timing Spark plug cables Ignition coil Condenser
	Defective fuel system	Starter system Fuel cock Carburetor mounting Clogged fuel lines Clogged fuel tank cap vent Carburetor
	Engine	Piston, rings, cylinders Crankshaft oil seals Cylinder head
Loss of power	Poor compression	Piston rings and cylinder Head gaskets Crankcase leaks

(continued)

8

Table 1   **TROUBLESHOOTING GUIDE** (continued)

Item	Problem or Cause	Things to Check
Loss of power (cont.)	Overheated engine	Lubricating oil supply Clogged cooling fins Oil pump Ignition timing Slipping clutch Carbon in combustion chamber
	Improper mixture	Dirty air cleaner Starter lever position Restricted fuel flow Gas cap vent hole
	Miscellaneous	Dragging brakes Tight wheel bearings Defective chain Clogged exhaust system
Gearshifting difficulties	Clutch	Adjustment Springs Friction plates Steel plates
	Transmission	Oil quantity Oil grade Return spring or pin Change lever or spring Drum position plate Change drum Change forks
Steering	Hard steering	Tire pressures Steering damper adjustment Steering stem head Steering head bearings Steering oil damper
	Pulls to one side	Unbalanced shock absorbers Drive chain adjustment Front/rear wheel alignment Unbalanced tires Defective swing arm Defective steering head
	Shimmy	Drive chain adjustment Loose or missing spokes Deformed rims Worn wheel bearings Wheel balance
Brakes	Poor brakes	Worn linings Brake adjustment Oil or water on brake linings Loose linkage or cables
	Noisy brakes	Worn or scratched lining Scratched brake drums Dirt in brake housing Disc distortion
	Unadjustable brakes	Worn linings Worn drums Worn brake cams

CHAPTER NINE

PERFORMANCE IMPROVEMENT

The history of Suzuki's three triple two-stroke street bikes, the GT380, GT550, and GT750, proves that Americans are not necessarily logical in their motorcycle preferences.

All three of these bikes have similar virtues. They are totally reliable, inexpensive to own, and they may be repaired inexpensively and easily when they do break. All of them have more than acceptable performance, not far short of today's crop of superbikes.

Yet, none of them ever became a big favorite of American bikers. This lack of appeal may have been due to their generally unexciting image, rather poor styling (at least on the earlier models), or simply the fact that American road riders have never been particularly fond of two-strokes.

Even the GT750, which for years was the best bargain available in the large-displacement touring bike field, never had more than a small hard-core group of admirers.

Yet, whatever the reason for their unpopularity, the bikes remain excellent choices for street machines, and will accept high performance modifications easily.

Many cyclists consider high performance to mean only one thing—more horsepower. Yet, if overall handling, reliability, and braking are not increased along with the power, a built-up motorcycle may become actively hazardous to ride.

High performance may also involve correcting model deficiencies. For example, all three GT-series Suzukis were equipped with marginal, high-wear shock absorbers (as were and are most Japanese motorcycles). Even the rider of a stone stocker may benefit from the installation of improved shocks under normal riding conditions.

Suspension modifications are particularly in order for the "Water Buffalo." Touring owners of the GT750, with their heavy-loaded, long-distance style of riding, will benefit greatly from such changes.

Performance modifications will be outlined on a step-by-step basis in this chapter, and it is suggested that this sequence be followed.

Since very few bike owners can afford to spend $500 and up for modifications at one time, they must build on a budget. Budget building is ideally suited to step-by-step modification. Following this outlined procedure keeps the outlay of money as low as possible, and ensures that each modification will give full benefits when it is made, rather than three steps down the road.

Since all three Suzukis have excellent engine performance within their respective displacement limitations, modifications to all three should begin by improving the bike's handling and braking.

SUSPENSION

It is senseless to think in terms of custom wheels, competition brake linings, gas-remote-reservoir shocks, and the rest if you are riding a worn-out bike.

Obviously, trick shocks will not improve handling if there is half an inch of side play in your swing arm due to worn-out bushings. Nor will aircaps improve fork performance if the steering head bearings are square.

So, just as with engine modification, suspension modification should begin with rebuilding the stock suspension system. Following the inspection procedures outlined in Chapter Seven, make sure that all components in the system fall well within allowable tolerances.

This is especially important on high-mileage machines, such as a touring GT750.

If stock components are worn out, they obviously should be the first to be replaced. However, in some cases, there is little point in using an OEM replacement when a heavier-duty, better-quality, and often lower-priced accessory part is available.

Swing Arm—All Models

One of the most frequent causes of poor handling is worn out swing arm bushings. Riders who feel that they can improve handling by replacing shocks or installing high performance fork kits or other expensive modifications will get nowhere if the swing arm has any side play whatsoever.

This should be checked by removing the rear wheel, and unbolting the shocks at their lower mount.

With the bike on its centerstand and braced, attempt to move the swing arm sideways. If there is *any* appreciable movement, the bushing should be replaced.

Rather than use the OEM part, a Target Products swing arm bushing kit should be used.

This consists of two extremely heavy replacement bushings, a shaft equipped with a lube fitting, and mounting bolts and washers.

Although the instructions say that this kit is a hand tool installation, the builder is strongly advised to have a power drill fitted with a reamer tip handy. It may be necessary to enlarge the swing arm to fit the new bushings. While this may be done with a circular file, it is slow and tedious.

The Target kit offers several advantages. Tolerances are far closer than stock swing arm to frame dimensions, so there is less possibility of wiggle. Secondly, the Target bushing will give better life than the stock part—it should last at least 25,000 miles before replacement. This kit is highly recommended for use on any GT-series Suzuki, and a necessity on a performance-modified machine.

Shocks—All Models

The stock rear shocks on all models of the GT Suzukis may be expected to last no more than 10,000 miles.

Unfortunately, although a lot has been written about worn-out shock absorbers, and how they adversely affect handling, no one has yet found a valid way for the average motorcyclist to check his shocks with common tools. Hand compression with the shocks off the machine and the springs removed proves nothing. Nor does "feel," since shocks go progessively bad, and most riders subconsciously adjust to this loss of handling without realizing it.

Two test methods exist, but unfortunately both of them are "feel" tests. The first is to have a friend, who is knowledgeable about shocks, try the machine through some dips, across some bumps, etc. Since this person will not be familiar with the machine, he may be able to tell if your shocks are worn out. Obviously, this method of testing is very subjective.

The second method is to have a friend ride behind you in a car or on a second bike, and watch the behavior of your shocks. If they pogo (repeatedly spring-return-spring-return) without any apparent damping, the shocks need replacement.

Also, there is a cynical rule of thumb which states that if you think your shocks are going bad, they are.

Rather than using OEM parts to replace worn-out shocks, it is highly recommended that quality aftermarket components be used.

These are frequently less expensive than the stock shocks, almost invariably have a longer lifespan, and always offer superior performance.

Since the GT380 and GT550 Suzukis are basically transportation machines, and seldom see continued use as streetrods or long distance touring bikes, probably the best shock to use is the extremely inexpensive, but very high quality, S&W shock absorber (**Figure 1**).

These give excellent damping performance on any bumps, and have a lifespan well in excess of 50,000 miles.

For solo riding on the GT380 or GT550, the S&W's should be equipped with 85-115 lb. dual-rate springs. For canyon riding or touring, 95-125 lb. springs should be used.

These shocks are also available for the GT750, although touring riders should consider installing S&W air adjustable shocks (**Figure 2**) instead.

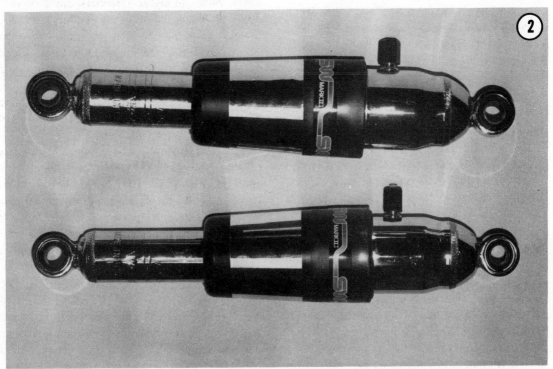

On the airshocks, the conventional springs are replaced with rubber airbags. Damping is standard oil hydraulic.

These rubber bags are pressurized to meet the rider's exact needs. With an almost-infinite variation, the rider can set the shocks for a soft, plush ride for long distance on the throughways, or stiff and exact for canyon travelling. The shocks can be adjusted for load conditions from single rider to two riders with full touring gear.

The rubber bags are protected by nylon sleeves, to prevent wear.

These airshocks may be equipped with an optional handlebar-mounted pressure gauge and a small syringe so that air pressure may be increased without having to look for a gas station air pump (**Figure 3**).

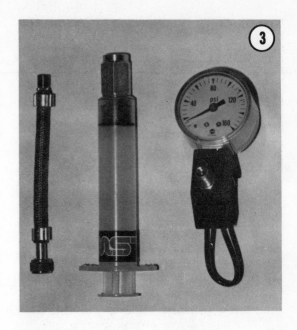

There are two differences between the airshocks and conventional shocks (besides their design): an airshock-equipped bike will sit approximately one inch lower at the rear than before; care must be taken that the shock is given proper clearance around chain guard, saddlebags, etc., when installed.

These airshocks (which are also available for the 380 and 550) are probably the most sensible for the 750 owner who needs a wide variance capability in his rear suspension.

Other recommended conventional shocks for the GT-series bikes are from Koni or Number One. Number One also offers a hydraulically-adjustable-ride shock for touring riders.

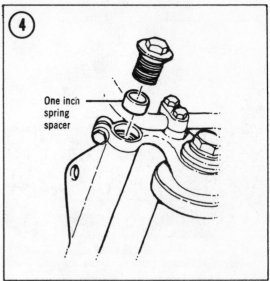

One inch spring spacer

Forks—All Models

While the stock front forks on the GT-series Suzukis rate as acceptable under "normal" riding circumstances, for performance riding or touring they are marginal.

Before modification, as with other components, the entire front end should be carefully inspected. Be especially attentive to abrasion marks on the fork legs or sliders, out-of-round or dry steering head bearings, insufficient or broken-down fork oil, and, most likely, worn-out fork springs.

The springs can be removed and measured against a new set of springs. If shorter than the new set, replace the old springs.

Even with a new set of springs, the front end will be somewhat undersprung, particularly if a fairing is mounted.

There are no heavy-duty fork springs available for the GT-series Suzukis, so the stock springs must be retained. Adding a one inch diameter shim inside the fork cap on each fork leg (**Figure 4**) will slightly preload the springs. The fork oil should be replaced with Torco 30-weight fork oil.

These changes will slightly improve spring preload and damping action.

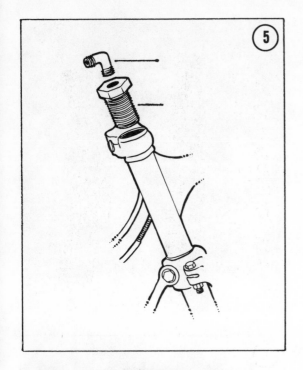

More significant improvement may be made by installing aircaps on the forks (available at most Suzuki dealers or by mail order from Suzuki City). These replace the stock caps, and permit pressurization of the fork internals. See **Figure 5**.

This accomplishes two things. First, it effectively preloads the forks, thus increasing spring poundage and ground clearance when cornering; it also decreases the possibility of seal leakage, since the air pressure forces the seals more tightly into position.

Normally, 8 to 10 pounds air pressure will be adequate loading for the performance or touring rider.

Wheels—All Models

Fully committed performance riders may wish to replace the stock wire wheels with cast alloy wheels.

Unsprung weight (those portions of the motorcycle affected directly by road shock, such as the swing arm, brakes, wheels, etc.) will be slightly reduced, and the new wheels will have greater rigidity. Both these changes will slightly improve handling.

More practical for the street rider, cast wheels vastly reduce motorcycle maintenance time, since there are no more spokes to clean, tighten, replace, etc.

The single drawback to cast wheels is cost— around $300 for a set of bare wheels and bearings.

The only cast wheels available for the GT-series bikes are from Morris Industries (**Figure 6**). On disc brake equipped front wheels, installation of the Morris wheels will require only removal of the front wheel, disassembly of the brake components and their reassembly onto the new wheel. The new wheel then bolts into place.

Drum brake equipped GT machines, though, must have the front drum replaced with a complete disc assembly. Most recommended is Suzuki's own system for the GS-series four-stroke bikes or, for those who want dual front discs, the entire GT750 kit. This kit must include both lower fork legs intended for the GT750, as the 380 and 550 lack mounting lugs for duals.

Also, it will be necessary to fabricate mounting hardware to mate the disc to the drum brake mounting lugs on 380's or 550's.

The addition of a second disc brake looks great, but Suzuki's single disc is more than efficient enough for normal and even mildly hard riding conditions.

Since the rear Morris Mag wheel has no provisions for the stock rear drum brake used on OEM wheels, an accessory rear disc system must be installed.

One solution to adding a rear disc is to purchase the complete Suzuki rear disc assembly used on the 1978 and later GS750C models. See **Figure 7**. The late-model GS rear brake uses

9

a smaller disc than the 1977, and is therefore far less prone to unexpected lockup. It will be necessary to use the GS brake pedal assembly and master cylinder, which will require welding mounting tabs to the frame.

Another solution is to install a complete Grimeca rear brake assembly (**Figure 8**). This consists of master cylinder, brake line, disc, and caliper, and may be ordered from Morris Industries for about $200. As with the Suzuki assembly, it will be necessary to build or have custom-built mounting hardware for the disc system.

Since the total expense of changing from wire wheels to cast wheels could be over $700, this is obviously too high for the average cyclist, especially considering the resale value of these bikes.

Brakes—All Models

Rear brake performance may be improved by replacing the stock linings with automotive metallic competition linings. Remove the stock brake shoes and take them to a high performance automotive brake shop. They will custom fit the metallic linings. However, this improvement will increase brake wear. Also, since less than 40% of braking involves the rear wheel, overall braking is not improved much; the stock Suzuki drum brakes do a satisfactory job of braking. This modification is only recommended for competition riders, who need all of the stopping power they can get.

Metallic linings can be fitted to the front drum brake. However, the four-leading-shoe drum used on the GT750's already delivers exceptional braking performance.

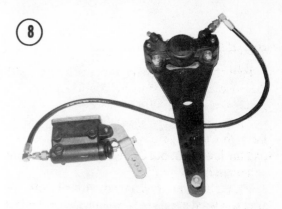

One important modification is to improve the performance of the late-model disc brakes in the rain. When it is wet, water collects on the disc. When the brake is applied, the puck hydroplanes ineffectively on the water surface for at least one full revolution. At this point, the rider generally squeezes harder on the brake lever. Since the water now has been cleaned from the disc, this excessive force often produces front wheel lockup—an extremely hazardous condition on wet pavement.

The solution is to remove the disc(s), and have it drilled (**Figure 9**). Drilling consists

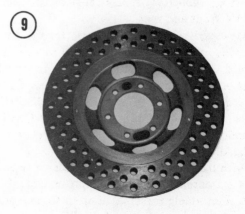

of punching many holes, up to ½ inch in diameter, through the disc. In the wet, the water will be squeezed from the disc into these holes, and the puck will not hydroplane.

This modification should not be made by an amateur machinist, since it is possible to mar the surface of the disc and ruin it, or make too many holes and weaken the disc (which will then possibly collapse under braking and lock up the wheel). These holes should be slightly countersunk on either side, to prevent the sharp edges from having a cheese grater effect on the puck.

This service may be done by an experienced competition machine shop, or by mail by Bill Bowman, Inc., for around $30 per disc.

Competition-oriented riders may also wish to have the disc faced (have its thickness reduced) to reduce the bike's unsprung weight. Again, this should not be done by the inexperienced, as it is quite easy to "chunk" the disc and ruin it (replacement discs cost well over $90).

Wheels—All Models

Rather than replacing the stock tires with OEM components when worn out, high-quality performance tires should be used.

Tires are a necessary compromise between the high-wear, high-adhesion racing compounds, and the low-wear, but decreased traction touring compounds.

Riders who are concerned with tire life, yet who still want excellent adhesion, should replace the stock rubber with identical-sized Michelin M45's, front and rear.

However, a better compromise for the performance rider (assuming that he is more concerned with handling than tire life) is to install a set of Continental Twins on his machine. Care should be taken to ensure that you get the RB2 front and the K112 rear, as the older Continentals are not noted for either their high-wear or handling qualities.

With the Continental Twins, a rider may expect extraordinary handling improvements (by test, comfortable cornering at up to 10 mph per corner) but also exceptional tire lifespan (front around 25,000 miles, rear 8,000 to 10,000 miles) depending on bike loading, riding conditions, road conditions, etc.

Other excellent performance tires are available from Goodyear, Pirelli, and Dunlop. The rider is advised to talk to other riders with the same bike and similar riding style who have used these or other tires.

Touring-oriented owners of the GT750 are advised against changing their rear wheel to the popular 16 inch diameter. Although this permits use of the comfortable large-diameter Harley-type tire, these compounds are more noted for their longevity than for maximum cornering adhesion.

ENGINE MODIFICATIONS

Although any of the three-cylinder Suzukis have excellent power, some riders may wish still greater performance. There may be more justification for this than simply the egotistical one of having the biggest gun on the block. The touring rider may wish to compensate for the increased loading of his machine and restore the bike's performance to unloaded stock levels. The commuting rider may wish more power for passing and throughway acceleration. Finally, the owner may ride with friends who have higher-performance machines and be tired of riding "Tail End Charlie" all the time.

Since Suzuki's engine design is reliable and strong, horsepower increases may be made without weakening the engine.

It is possible to build either of the three engines to produce much more horsepower. However, this will be at the expense of rideability. Even more than a four-stroke engine, a built-up two-stroke will be peaky and hard to ride. Heavy power increases involve port modification, which makes the power band narrower and higher in the rpm range, much like a roadracing bike. The modifier is advised to move cautiously before making major changes.

The owner of a GT-series Suzuki is advised to be conservative, even though various, rather fascinating bits of exotica are available for all three models. For the 380 and 550, replacement cylinders are available from England. These increase displacement, radically alter port timing, and convert the engine to water cooling. However, these are not recommended, for several reasons. For U.S. owners, they are not readily available, and spare parts may be even

9

scarcer. Another consideration is the expense of these parts. Finally, consider the difficulty of finding expert help should you run into trouble.

Super performance parts have also been manufactured for the GT750, originally for their use in small-size racing automobiles. But, as with the water-jacket big-bore barrels for the smaller triples, these parts should be considered carefully before purchase.

Oviously, these parts will be expensive. And the street-riding performance builder should consider that these parts were intended for racing application. Racers will accept parts which last no more than a few races, so long as they significantly increase power. But the street rider must consider reliability, since he is hardly likely to tear his bike down every thousand miles or so. A final caution is that racing-only parts usually develop gobs of horsepower, but only within the powerband needed for competition. Since the street rider spends most of his time riding at low- and mid-rpm, a competition modification would not be suitable.

Pre-modification—GT750

Before any engine modifications are made to the GT750, the crankshaft seals should be closely inspected. If worn (particularly likely on early or high-mileage Water Buffaloes), they should be replaced with the late-model seals, which are fitted with metal flanges.

Since installation of these seals is a press-fit machine-shop job, it is recommended that the work be done by a competent agency rather than the owner.

Head Milling—All Models

Since all three Suzukis have extremely low compression ratios, horsepower may be moderately increased, without any sacrifices being made in reliability or longevity, by increasing the engine's compression.

This is done by removing the head and milling 1mm from the base, thus slightly reducing the combustion chamber's area. For still further performance, up to 3mm may be milled from the GT750's head without any problems being created.

This work may be done by any competent machine shop or by most Suzuki agencies with machining facilities. Mail order modifications of this type may be done through Suzuki City.

With 1mm removed from the head, compression should be increased to an ideal 150-160 lb.

Barrel Change—GT380

In 1976, the GT380's barrels were modified, and two additional transfer ports were added. Performance-oriented owners of pre-1976 models would be advised to replace their older model barrels with the higher-performance late-model part.

This is a simple replacement operation, to stock specifications, and requires no modifications.

Ram Air—GT380

Performance may be increased, as already mentioned in the section on suspension, by an overall reduction in the bike's weight. Some owners of GT380's have attempted to cut their bike's weight by removing the cast Ram Air shroud from the engine.

This should not be done under any circumstances, since the Ram Air is an extremely functional and necessary cooling device. The cooler a two-stroke engine runs, the more horsepower it develops. The removal of the shrouding, even though it decreases bike weight, will actually decrease performance through a horsepower loss.

Competition builders may wish to go to the trouble of removing the shroud and replacing it with a far lighter, but still functional, sheet metal shroud. This should be hand-bent to match the contours of the stock Ram Air shroud.

Oil Pump Modification
or Removal—All Models

Most competition-only two-strokes use premixed oil and gas rather than the separate oil tank with pump system used on the GT-series Suzukis. This saves weight and eliminates the disastrous consequences of an oil injection failure. However, it should not be done on any street GT machine. Having to mix gas and oil at every roadside stop is time consuming and messy.

Port Modification—All Models

According to theory, port alteration on a two-stroke engine is quite simple. If you widen the intake and exhaust ports, you merely increase the mixture amount and therefore performance without altering the timing. If you raise the intake ports 2mm and raise the exhaust ports 2mm, you will get more power at high rpm without making much of a sacrifice at lower rpm.

Since the theory seems so simple, some builders buy a Dremel tool, a handful of tips, and go after performance. More often than not, the end result is reduced performance and a bike with an unusable or totally impractical powerband.

A two-stroke is deceptive in its simplicity. Without valves, camshafts, etc., modification should be simple.

But even though the engine is simple in its component parts, in function, things are not nearly that uncomplicated. Each part of the two-stroke engine interacts with the parts to affect the engine's behavior. What appears to be a minor change can severely alter the engine performance.

Engine port modification is possibly the most critical area of all. Any changes should be made cautiously and only by an experienced builder.

In spite of many cycle magazine articles that cheerily tell you how to do your own porting, this work should only be done by an experienced two-stroke porting service, such as Don Vesco Yamaha or Suzuki City.

Generally, it is possible to find a local porting service that has a successful racetrack reputation. However, the buyer should still be wary— a competition porter may automatically think in terms too radical for a street bike, and produce an engine with a powerband impossible for normal street conditions.

The rider interested in increased performance through port alteration is well advised to consult the chosen porting service directly, and specify quite exactly what improvements he wants and what sacrifices he is willing to make.

Small improvements in performance may be gained by removing the barrels and smoothing the edges of the ports. This work should only be done with emery paper or sandpaper, by hand. No power tools should be used, to prevent the possibility of inadvertent engine damage. It is especially critical that the angle of the port edges not be altered, since these are carefully designed to be the way they are, generally to reduce engine noise.

Exhaust—All Models

The stock exhaust systems used on the Suzuki triples are, like all OEM systems, a necessary compromise between unit cost, maximum power output, and legal noise limits.

Since an unmuffled two-stroke engine is one of the loudest and most irritating noises known, extreme care is taken to properly silence exhaust noise. For competition purposes only, significant power may be gained by installing a custom-built exhaust system with stinger tip.

This should not be done under any circumstances on street-ridden bikes, though. Motorcycles are already under the governmental gun for noise pollution as it is. Each unmuffled or racing-exhaust-equipped street bike significantly increases the probability of more restrictive and possibly totally anti-motorcycle legislation. Riders who value their sport, and wish to continue being able to participate in it, must exert a high degree of social responsibility.

There is another excellent reason to avoid high noise level exhaust systems on the street. A primary cause of fatigue is noise. The louder a motorcycle is, the less time you can ride it comfortably. For touring riders this is highly significant, since the long distance biker must have the option of being able to put down long miles without exhausting himself.

The only street exhaust for any of the Suzuki triples which can be recommended is the three-into-one system manufactured by Strader Engineering (**Figure 10**).

Installation of this system is bolt-on, and should not require carburetor rejetting.

9

Power will be noticeably increased in the mid-range, which will be of the greatest benefit to the street rider, and the bike's overall weight will be reduced by well over 20 lb.

Even a non-performance-oriented rider might wish to install the Strader system when his stock exhaust rusts out, due to the extremely high cost of the OEM replacement.

Though the Strader exhaust is generally legal, the rider will find that noise level is slightly increased. For this reason, the rider who is primarily concerned with touring is best advised to stay with the stock system, for comfort's sake.

Owners of pre-1974 GT750's may consider replacing their exhaust system with a later stock exhaust. This later system eliminates the cross-over tubes, and therefore allows the engine to put out slightly greater power through the mid-range. Obviously, the noise level will not be increased.

A less expensive change on the pre-1974 GT750's is to simply remove the crossover tubes and plug the holes in the pipe with appropriately-sized automotive freeze plugs. This is not only a temporary change, but an extremely ugly one.

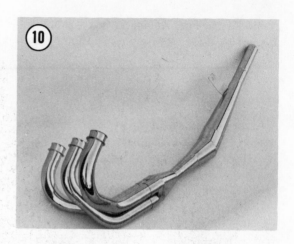

Air Filter—All Models

Intake flow may be increased by replacing the stock air filter element with a stock-dimensioned filter from K&N.

Some riders feel that performance will be increased by entirely removing the air cleaner assembly, and installing vacuum stacks (air-horns, bellhorns, etc.). This is certainly not recommended for street riders, due to the likelihood of sucking engine-damaging contaminants directly into the engine.

Carburetor Change—GT380

After head milling and possibly mild port modification, the GT380's intake capability will be greater than the stock carburetors permit.

The entire 24mm carburetor assembly may be removed and replaced with the 28mm set of Mikunis used stock on the GT550. This modification is an easy bolt-on.

Rejetting the carburetors should not be necessary when they are installed on a modified 380, since the 550's baseline jetting should be ideal on the modified smaller engine.

But since carburetors see a lot of unauthorized and amateur jetting, baseline main jet sizing on these carburetors should be 95 mains on the center cylinder and 97.5 mains on the outer two carburetors.

With these carburetors installed, performance will remain close to stock on the low end, gradually improving through the midrange, and of greatest benefit in the upper rpm range.

Carburetor Change—GT550

A mildly modified GT550 may also have its performance increased by replacing the stock carburetors with three 32mm slide-needle Mikunis (**Figure 11**). It is recommended that these be ordered as a closely pre-jetted kit from Suzuki City.

Many riders find the expense of such a kit too great, and attempt to set up their own carburetors from off-the-shelf or used carburetors. However, the slide-needle Mikuni is an extremely complex carburetor with a huge array of available modifications and overlapping functions. With replacement slides running close to $10, and main jets at $5 each, it takes very few jetting changes to make the cost of a self-set-up kit higher than that of a pre-jetted kit.

In addition, of course, the inexperienced tuner runs the excellent possibility of ruining his

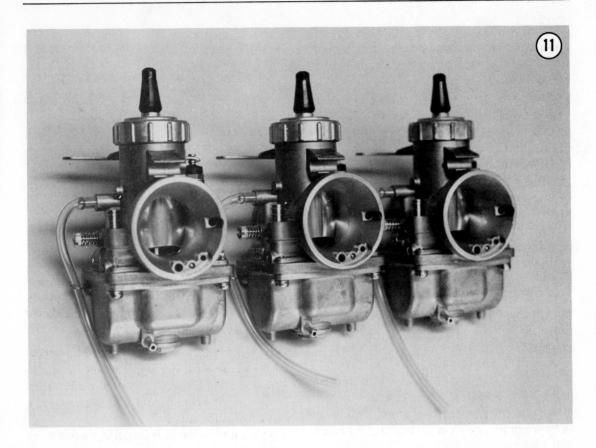

engine when setting up such a carburetor from scratch.

When the GT550 carburetors are changed, the stock throttle cable must be replaced with an early (pre-CV carburetor model) cable from a GT750.

Carburetor Change—GT750

With a mildly modified 750 engine, engine performance may be still further increased by replacing the stock carburetors with a set of 34mm Mikunis. As with the recommended carburetor change on the GT550, these carburetors should be purchased as a prejetted kit (for example, the kit available from Suzuki City) rather than off-the-shelf.

Installed on a pre-1974 GT750, these carburetors will keep low end performance at pre-modified levels, improve midrange moderately, and give significant boosts to top end performance.

Even greater benefits are possible when the Mikunis are used on 1974-later GT's. The stock constant-vacuum carburetors are known for reliability and economy. However, they have two major drawbacks for the performance enthusiast—they are sluggish in their response to engine demands and they offer less than maximum flow. After the CV carburetors are replaced with the larger slide-needle mixers, engine performance will be boosted throughout the engine's range (still most noticeably at high rpm).

With these carburetors installed on early GT's, mileage may drop 2-4 mpg, depending on riding style. On the bikes formerly equipped with CV carburetors, mileage may drop as much as 6-8 mpg. But since the Water Buffalo has a large tank and is economical, performance oriented riders will not have any trouble adjusting to the loss.

It is possible to modify the stock air cleaner assembly connectors on CV-carburetor GT750's for use with the slide-needle carburetors. But on earlier models it will be necessary to remove the entire air cleaner assembly and use three separate K&N or Filtron air cleaners (**Figure 12**) mounted directly to the carburetor bellmouths.

Ignition Change—All Models

There is little point in increasing the intake and exhaust efficiency if the ignition system remains at stock levels.

The performance-oriented builder should plan for ignition modification as the final step in his street hop-up.

Stock coils are rated at only 10,000-12,000 volts. These should be replaced with heavy-duty, high-output components.

An excellent choice are the Lucas high performance coils, easily recognized by their blue anodized body. In spite of the somewhat vile reputation that Lucas components have (primarily caused by the low-cost, low-reliability parts used as stock on most British bikes), these high performance coils will provide noticeable power improvements and excellent reliability. They are a wire-in replacement, and do not require modification to the ignition circuitry.

A second coil option is to install three 6-volt coils in place of the stock 12-volt components. With these installed, voltage will be increased. However, it will be necessary to wire a ballast resistor (such as that found stock on the Kawasaki Z-1) into circuit between the battery and coil, to prevent overdriving and frying the smaller-voltage parts.

The second change to the ignition circuit is to replace the very poor OEM ignition condenser with a higher-quality U.S.-built part. Any automotive ignition condenser rated at around 20 microfarads will be ideal.

Finally, care should be taken to use only Suzuki OEM points and points plate assemblies. Too many of the accessory points assemblies have a thin backing plate or insufficiently strong springs. Either of these will produce plate distortion or points bounce, causing an erratic firing sequence at high rpm.

OVERALL

If performance modifications are made sensibly and relatively conservatively, the performance of the GT-series Suzukis can be significantly increased, without loss in reliability and rideability. In addition, suspension modifications make the bikes far better suited to the needs of American riders, and much more fun to ride.

(12)

Table 1   PERFORMANCE MANUFACTURERS AND SERVICES

Manufacturer	Service
Bill Bowman, Inc. 2546 Manhattan Ave. Montrose, Calif. 91020	Disc drilling and facing
Don Vesco Yamaha 765 El Cajon Blvd. El Cajon, Calif. 92020	Porting
Morris Industries 2901 W. Garry Ave. Santa Ana, Calif. 92704	Cast wheels, disc brake components
S&W Engineered Products 2617 Woodland Dr. Anaheim, Calif. 92801	Shock absorbers
Strader Engineering 7358 Deering Canoga Park, Calif. 91303	Exhaust systems
Suzuki City 728 S. La Brea Ave. Inglewood, Calif. 90301	Head milling, porting, performance parts, custom engine building
Target Products 2724 W. Main Alhambra, Calif. 91801	Swing arm bushing kit

9

APPENDIX

SPECIFICATIONS

This chapter contains specifications and performance figures for the various Suzuki models covered by this book. The tables are arranged in order of increasing engine size.

SPECIFICATIONS, MODEL GT380

DIMENSIONS
Length — 82.9 inches
Width — 33.5 inches
Wheelbase — 53.4 inches
Road clearance — 6.1 inches
Weight — 377 pounds

PERFORMANCE
Maximum speed — 105-110 mph
Braking distance (feet/mph) — 46 ft at 30 mph

ENGINE
Bore and stroke (inches) — 2.13 by 2.13
            (millimeters) — 54 by 54
Displacement (cubic inches) — 22.6
            (cubic centimeters) — 371
Compression ratio — 6.7 to 1
Horsepower/rpm — 38 at 7,500
Torque (foot-pounds/rpm) — 28.4 at 6,000

FUEL SYSTEM
Carburetors — Three VM24SC
Fuel tank capacity — 3.3 US gallons

LUBRICATION SYSTEM
Type — Suzuki CCI
Oil tank capacity — 3.2 US pints

IGNITION SYSTEM
Type — Battery and coil
Ignition timing (degrees BTDC) — 24
Spark plug — NGK B-7ES

TRANSMISSION
Primary reduction ratio — 2.833 to 1
Gear ratios
    1st — 2.333 to 1
    2nd — 1.500 to 1
    3rd — 1.157 to 1
    4th — 0.904 to 1
    5th — 0.782 to 1
    6th — 0.708 to 1

FRAME
Steering angle — 40 degrees right and left
Caster — 62 degrees
Trail — 4.3 inches
Tire size
    Front — 3.00-19
    Rear — 3.50-18

BRAKES
Type — Internal expanding
Diameter
    Front — 7 inches
    Rear — 7 inches

10

SPECIFICATIONS, MODEL GT550

DIMENSIONS
  Length   85.0 inches
  Width   33.5 inches
  Wheelbase   55.3 inches
  Road clearance   5.9 inches
  Weight   412 pounds

PERFORMANCE
  Maximum speed   110-115 mph
  Climing ability   26 degrees

ENGINE
  Bore and stroke (inches)   2.40 by 2.44
               (millimeters)   61 by 62
  Displacement (cubic inches)   33.2
            (cubic centimeters)   544
  Compression ratio   6.8 to 1
  Horsepower/rpm   50 at 6,500
  Torque (foot-pounds/rpm)   44.1 at 5,000

FUEL SYSTEM
  Carburetors   Three VM32SC or BS40
  Fuel tank capacity   4.5 US gallons

LUBRICATION SYSTEM
  Type   Suzuki CCI
  Oil tank capacity   3.2 US pints

IGNITION SYSTEM
  Type   Battery and coil
  Ignition timing (degrees BTDC)   24
  Spark plug   NGK B-7ES

TRANSMISSION
  Primary reduction ratio   2.242 to 1
  Gear ratios
    1st   2.864 to 1
    2nd   1.736 to 1
    3rd   1.363 to 1
    4th   1.125 to 1
    5th   0.923 to 1

FRAME
  Steering angle   42 degrees left and right
  Caster   61 degrees
  Trail   4.6 inches
  Tire size
    Front   3.25-19
    Rear   4.00-18

BRAKES
  Type   Internal expanding and disc
  Diameter
    Front   7 3/4 inches
    Rear   7 3/4 inches

SPECIFICATIONS, MODEL GT750

DIMENSIONS	
Length	87.2 inches
Width	34.0 inches
Wheelbase	57.8 inches
Road clearance	5.5 inches
Weight	482 pounds
PERFORMANCE	
Maximum speed	115-120 mph
Braking distance (feet/mph)	46 feet at 30 mph
ENGINE	
Bore and stroke (inches)	2.76 by 2.52
(millimeters)	70 by 64
Displacement (cubic inches)	45.0
(cubic centimeters)	738
Compression ratio	6.7 to 1
Horsepower/rpm	67 at 6,500
Torque (foot-pounds/rpm)	55.7 at 5,500
FUEL SYSTEM	
Carburetors	Three VM32SC or BS40
Fuel tank capacity	4.5 US gallons
LUBRICATION SYSTEM	
Type	Suzuki CCI
Oil tank capacity	3.2 US pints
IGNITION SYSTEM	
Type	Battery and Coil
Ignition timing (degrees BTDC)	24
Spark plugs	NGK B-7ES
TRANSMISSION	
Primary reduction ratio	1.673 to 1
Gear ratios	
1st	2.846 to 1
2nd	1.736 to 1
3rd	1.363 to 1
4th	1.125 to 1
5th	0.923 to 1
FRAME	
Steering angle	40 degrees right and left
Caster	63 degrees
Trail	3.74 inches
Tire size	
Front	3.25-19
Rear	4.00-18
BRAKES	
Type	Internal expanding and disc
Diameter	
Front	7¾ inches
Rear	7¾ inches

10

INDEX

NOTES

Do-It-Yourself Boat Maintenance

The world's largest publisher of automotive and motorcycle manuals now offers a complete line of maintenance and tune-up handbooks for owners of sailboats, powerboats, outboard motors, stern drive units, and small inboard engines.

Each title features step-by-step procedures for maintaining and repairing the hull, fittings, interior, electrical systems, plumbing, galley equipment, and the countless other items that keep boat owners busy.

As in all Clymer handbooks, the expert text and detailed photos and illustrations will put money-saving maintenance well within the reach of anyone reasonably handy with tools.

The titles listed below are available through your local bookstore, marine outlet, or postpaid direct from Clymer Publications.

SAILBOAT MAINTENANCE . . . . (B600) $9.00

POWERBOAT MAINTENANCE . . . . (B620) $9.00

BRITISH SEAGULL OUTBOARDS, 1.5 TO 6 HP . . . . (B660) $8.00

CHRYSLER OUTBOARDS, 3.5 TO 20 HP, 1966-1977 . . . (B655) $8.00

CHRYSLER OUTBOARDS, 25 TO 135 HP, 1966-1977 . . . (B657) $8.00

EVINRUDE OUTBOARDS, 1.5 TO 33 HP, 1965-1977 . . . (B644) $8.00

EVINRUDE OUTBOARDS, 40 TO 140 HP, 1965-1977 . . . (B647) $8.00

JOHNSON OUTBOARDS, 1.5 TO 33 HP, 1965-1977 . . . (B663) $8.00

JOHNSON OUTBOARDS, 40 TO 140 HP, 1965-1977 . . . (B665) $8.00

MERCURY OUTBOARDS, 4 TO 40 HP, 1964-1977 . . . . (B650) $8.00

MERCURY OUTBOARDS, 50 TO 150 HP, 1964-1977 . . . (B653) $8.00

SAILBOAT AUXILIARY ENGINES (Atomic, Chrysler, Ford, Perkins, Pisces, Volvo-Penta, Westerbeke, and Yanmar) . . . . (B610) $9.00

STERN DRIVE UNITS (OMC, MerCruiser, Volvo, Stern-Powr, Berkeley, and Jacuzzi) . . . . (B641) $9.00

CLYMER PUBLICATIONS

12860 MUSCATINE STREET • P.O. BOX 20 • ARLETA, CALIFORNIA 91331